Five Arguments All Couples (Need To) Have

Joanna Harrison is an experienced couple therapist, former divorce lawyer, wife and mother, all of which have led her to conclude that relationships are hard work, and that we all need all the help we can get. She is a senior clinician at Tavistock Relationships and also works as a consultant to parents and separating couples at Family Law in Partnership.

Five Arguments All Couples (Need To) Have

And why the washing-up matters

JOANNA HARRISON

SOUVENIR
PRESS

First published in Great Britain in 2022 by
Souvenir Press,
an imprint of PROFILE BOOKS LTD
29 Cloth Fair
London
EC1A 7JQ
www.souvenirpress.co.uk

10 9 8 7 6 5 4 3 2 1

Typeset in Freight Text by MacGuru Ltd
Printed and bound in Great Britain by Clays Ltd, Elcograf S.p.A.

A CIP record for this book can be obtained from the British Library

ISBN 978 1 78816 726 0
eISBN 978 1 78283 814 2

FSC
www.fsc.org
MIX
Paper from
responsible sources
FSC® C018072

To Rupert, you've made this book
possible in so many ways

'The opposite to love is not hate. These two always co-exist so long as there is a live relationship. The opposite to love is indifference.'

Henry Dicks, 1967

'If we choose to live with someone in an intimate relationship – whether of the opposite or the same sex, whether legal spouses or not – we are confronted with the problems of sharing space, physical and mental.'

Ronald Britton, 2003

'I hope husbands and wives will continue to debate and
    combat
over everything debatable and combatable,
Because I believe a little incompatibility is the spice of life.'

From 'I do, I will, I have', Ogden Nash

Contents

Introduction

A couple in therapy were talking about their new mattress. One of them liked to sleep on a hard mattress, and one liked to sleep on a soft mattress, and they were happy that they had recently found a mattress that could work for both of them, hard on one side, and soft on the other. They laughed and said 'If only our relationship could be like that – where we could both have it our way without having to argue or make any compromises with each other.'

I've worked in the field of couple relationships since 2004, first as a family lawyer and then as a couple therapist, and I've heard many arguments that couples have as they try to deal with loving and living with someone different from themselves. I've also seen them find different ways to resolve frustrations and tensions, sometimes finding a way to manage them within the relationship, sometimes thinking that separating is the answer. But I've yet to find a perfect mattress version of a relationship, where everyone gets their own way – so quit now if that's what you're hoping this book will offer you.

What I do hope to offer you is a sense that you are not alone when you argue with your partner about certain things. And also, by showing you snapshots of my experiences with couples,* I want to help you to understand what your arguments might really be about, so that you can make better use of them, stop having them so often and recover from them better. And crucially, if you have children, to improve the environment in which they are growing up. (Even if you are separated, it is still important to think about how the way you relate to each other might impact your children.)

The five arguments
Over the years of working with couples, I've noticed that there are five areas which come up again and again as areas of tension (areas that are also familiar to me from my own relationship and from the relationships I see and hear about in the world around me).

These five areas are what is meant by the 'five arguments' in the title. I could have called them 'The Five Areas Couples Often End Up Having to Navigate With Each Other Throughout Their Whole Relationship' but it wasn't quite as catchy.

---

*The case studies in the book are all fictional but are inspired by my experiences working with people on their relationships. For more details of my approach and my working context, see Appendix 1.

These are:

- *How we communicate with each other.*
- *How we deal with each other's families.*
- *How we deal with sharing out all the jobs that need doing.*
- *How we manage distance between us.*
- *How we feel about each other's bodies.*

I think of these five 'arguments' as being the inevitable consequences of sharing space with each other in a relationship – space that is not only physical but also mental. Each 'argument' has its own chapter. We need to find ways to communicate about the space we share (chapter 1). We need to understand what we each bring into the space from our family, culture and history (chapter 2). We need to work out who is going to do what when it comes to the work required to manage our space (chapter 3). We need to figure out how we manage distance within our joint space (chapter 4). And we need to think about how our bodies relate to each other in the space we share (chapter 5).

There's also a chapter for couples who become parents (chapter 6), because having a child or children in this shared space can make all these areas of tension more complicated. Chapter 7 looks at endings to relationships, and chapter 8 discusses the idea of getting professional help for your relationship.

Rather than thinking that arguments or difficult conversations are to be avoided at all costs, some offer a relationship the potential to grow. When we come up against each other's different ideas, we have an opportunity to learn about the things we both care about and to learn more mutually agreeable ways of doing things (as well as learn where each other's limits are). I find this idea conveyed vividly by the Japanese art of mending broken pottery known as kintsugi, which celebrates and draws attention to the breakages and repair of an object. Repair is so important. If we can better understand what is going on between us in our relationships when we argue, and repair with each other after we argue, it can give us an opportunity to strengthen our relationships and to get closer to each other.

I am not at all encouraging or advocating arguments that get out of hand, or that pose risk to the people arguing. Some arguments are hostile, risky, dangerous, out of control or violent. If you are at risk or feel as if you might be at risk in your relationship, or if there is sustained conflict that never gets resolved, then it is important that you seek direct help. We know that frequent, intense and poorly resolved conflict can harm children, which makes getting help crucial. Appendix 2 lists resources to which you can turn.

Is this book just for couples who argue? We don't argue, so why is this book applicable to us?

Of course, if the differences of ideas between you don't cause you any trouble or stress, then maybe you've found a way of accepting everything about each other – and that's great. But it isn't always the case that couples who don't argue have no tensions to deal with. Keeping silent about issues may mean that resentment builds up or may result in a loss of connection or a withdrawal from each other. So even if you don't argue, there may be some important areas covered in this book that relate to your situation.

Why the washing-up matters

Sometimes – well, often – the themes of these five arguments express themselves in disagreements or arguments about seemingly small things. Couples often seem to worry about whether it is appropriate to bring their issues about domestic matters to therapy – an argument about the washing-up, or towels left on the bed, or what happened when one of them took a shower. (I hear about showers often, particularly from parents, perhaps because it can become surprisingly complicated to have a shower when you have a small baby.)

When it comes to washing-up, I have heard it all. When to do it, when not to do it. Why won't you do it, or why won't you just leave it? Disagreements about how best to stack the dishwasher. Why do you leave bits in the plug? Why don't you rinse the cloth? The tension in these arguments helps couples define themselves as separate people, and there can be a playfulness to it. Without the inherent incompatibility of some ideas, life could get rather boring (at least that is Ogden Nash's view, as in the quote at the front). But sometimes it's important to look at this day-to-day stuff at a deeper level, which is why I never get bored hearing about it.

So much of our lives together as a couple plays out at the level of the familiar daily stuff. We may see a shoe left in the middle of the room and in a split second see it as a representation of our partner's attitude, or their ideas about something (whether or not we've got it right). And while the backdrop of our lives is familiar, there can also be a less familiar layer attached to it. Our deeper fears and frustrations, and the things we may find it difficult to express openly with each other, can often express themselves in the domestic world around us. We ourselves – let alone our partners – may not be conscious of this deeper layer, and so part of the work of being in a relationship is becoming more aware of these more hidden aspects. If, when I am working with a couple, we can understand something about why they had a row about the washing-up or why it is a place of conflict between them, then perhaps we can learn something important about them and see what might need attention in their relationship. My work is often to try to explore those meanings with a couple.

Take Ashley and Evie. Ashley has left his plate in the sink without washing it. Evie thinks it should be washed as soon as it is used. This is something that they argue about – quite often in fact, given how often the washing-up needs doing. If we think about it only as an argument about plates and sinks it might just seem like a storm in a teacup (just to bring more crockery into it). But if we were to look at it through a different lens, there could be significant aspects to understand. It could say something important about Evie's more general feelings about the division of labour in their relationship. Or perhaps it could be a sign that they aren't good at communicating with each other in a productive or thoughtful way about things that need to be done. Perhaps it reflects the way things have been done in the different households in which they've grown up. Perhaps it touches some particular nerve in them that they don't yet understand. Though both of them may feel there is a 'right' way to do it, this becomes irrelevant now they are in a relationship; what is more important is that they find a way that feels manageable because it's something they have to deal with every day. With each chapter I hope to offer a different lens on what could be going on if you're arguing about the washing-up.

How to use this book
I'm not in the least suggesting that you use this book to deconstruct every argument you have, whether or not it's about washing the dishes. While I may have the opportunity to think about a couple's conflicts in detail, a therapy room is a very particular space in which this can be done, sometimes painstakingly, with the help of a thinking observer. Life outside a therapy room is different and you can't spend hours deconstructing everything. But I hope to share some of the thinking from inside the consulting room to give you a wider range of possibilities to consider as reasons for the tensions you have with your partner (as opposed to them just being irrational and annoying about petty things). The presentation of the couples in the book may differ in lots of ways from your own personal experiences and circumstances, but I hope that there will be aspects from which you can extrapolate and reflect upon in relation to your own situation.

I use the word 'you' throughout. Sometimes I may be voicing things as if speaking to someone in an existing relationship, or even both people, but this book isn't just for you if you're in a relationship. It may offer a perspective on a relationship you've been in but are in no longer, or you may want to learn some more about what goes on within relationships.

Throughout the book there are ideas for you to reflect on either personally, or, if you are in a relationship, to think about together. Whether you both read the book is a matter for discussion. There is no right answer, but I do know that it probably isn't helpful for one of you to read it and use it as a way of telling your partner what's wrong with your relationship (or with them!) without giving them a chance to read it too.

Reading about this sensitive topic of our private lives can stir up issues. I am reminded of the time I came home having been talking with a couple about an argument over putting the bins out. The first thing I did was get cross with my own husband about the bins not being out. Often reading or hearing about themes sensitises us (as when we learn a new word and then somehow hear it three times in a week), so go gently on yourself and your partner if the issues in the book seem to hit a nerve or ring true. If they do, then perhaps it is a sign that these need attending to. If it feels too difficult or sensitive to reflect together on some of the issues presented here, then that may be a sign that therapy could be a safer way to do this, in a space with a third person. There's advice in chapter 8 about how you might think about getting help from a therapist.

Where is the love?
I realise that I haven't mentioned the word 'love' yet. It seems to me that couples can get to feeling more loving

with each other when they can attend to some of these core five issues. When it comes to love, figuring out a way to deal with the tensions, even if they are only about the washing-up, matters. This is the version of love that is about hard work rather than magically living happily ever after because you are perfectly compatible.

This hard work isn't just a case of making sure that you have a date night or that there are occasional bunches of flowers or cups of tea (though these things can have real value). The real work, as I hope to illustrate, is in trying to hear and understand each other better, and in doing so, figure out something that works well enough for you both. (This will also inevitably involve coping with disappointments about things that you can't get to work in the way you hoped.) Rather than offering a manual full of advice where I tell you what to do and what not to do, I hope the chapters that follow can provide a set of extra lenses for increasing understanding of yourselves and each other, and of what the hard work of relating to each other better might involve.

So, let's go ...

1

Communication (aka 'you never listen to me')

I'm seeing a new couple for the first time. They sit in the chairs in my consulting room and we introduce ourselves. 'So,' I say, 'perhaps we could start by thinking about what it is that has brought you here today.'

One of them starts. 'Well, I suppose what we are really struggling with is communication.'

His partner nods. 'It's like we always get in a knot. We can't seem to have conversations about things without getting cross with each other. Even the small things.'

Like so many of the couples who have sat in the same chairs as these two, the issue of communication is at the top of the list of things they want help with. Couples tell me they have difficulties such as:

- they don't seem to be on the same page as each other, or they misread each other
- they can't talk to each other at all about anything difficult
- if they do talk to each other then it turns into a less

constructive kind of conversation where they are full of anger or upset, or

- once the conversation has become angry or upset, they can't get back on track.

It's early days, but my work with this couple will be to help them look at what they are struggling with and to try to explore whatever it is from new angles – which is easier for me to do since I am not them, and from where I'm sitting I can see in real time the way in which they communicate. By thinking about the problems they have with this, we may work together to find a way of communicating that works better for them.

I'm clearly not sitting in real time with you. However, by showing you some of the ways that some couples struggle with this area, I hope to give you new angles from which to think about the ways in which you communicate in your relationship. In order to have any of the 'arguments you (need to) have' productively, you are going to need to think about communication, so it seems to me appropriate for this to be the subject of the first chapter.

You never listen to me!

A regular complaint from people I work with is that their partner doesn't listen to them, and that their partner can't seem to hear what they are saying, even though they feel as if they've been telling them something 'for years'. Sometimes I ask them what being listened to would be like and it seems that their idea of being listened to might mean having things their way; that if their partner would agree with them, then they would feel like they had been heard. But the two things aren't the same. Being listened to by your partner isn't the same as being agreed with (just as listening to them isn't the same as agreeing with them). Nevertheless, there is a huge value, often underestimated, in being able to listen to each other helpfully. What seems more important than someone getting their own way is actually there being enough room for each partner's different feelings and views to be aired. This creates a starting point from which to agree a decision or outcome mutually.

Here's an example of a very familiar dynamic that often stops couples having the conversation they need to have.

Sarah and Tomas are a couple in their late twenties who have been together for a couple of years. Their lease is up and they are thinking about where to live. One of the options is further away from where they both work centrally. This situation is bringing up different worries for them.

SARAH: I really don't want to live an hour away from work even if it does mean we can try and save a bit more.

TOMAS: Oh, I'm not worried about that. I honestly think you'd get used to it in no time. I really think that financially it makes sense.

SARAH: But I find it stressful enough commuting thirty minutes, let alone double that.

TOMAS: I really think you would find it okay. Loads of people manage it. It'll make such a difference to have less rent to pay.

SARAH: I wish you could listen to me!

TOMAS: What do you mean?!

If we stop and pause just here at this point in the conversation, it's starting to feel as if they are getting into a battle of ideas. Both of them have relevant concerns, but neither is feeling that their concerns are being heard by the other, and neither is showing the other that the other's concerns have been heard. Sarah seems to have started to panic that Tomas isn't listening to her and isn't registering her worry. She is now getting upset:

SARAH: Why can you never see it from my point of view? I suppose it's your way or nothing.

TOMAS: No! That's not what I mean. Can you just chill out?

SARAH: No! I don't want to chill out! Can you just try to see it from my point of view!

TOMAS: I really don't think that the journey time should be the main factor – you'll get used to it. It's normal for lots of people to commute that far.

SARAH: Oh well I'm sorry I'm not normal. Fine, we'll do it your way.

TOMAS: Why do you always have to get so angry about things? It's impossible to talk to you.

Both of them are getting more irritable as the conversation goes on. If I was working in therapy with them, I'd ask them to pause at this moment and reflect on where the conversation is going, to notice the intensifying emotion and to think about how to slow it down. It seems that Sarah is getting more and more anxious that Tomas doesn't see her point of view and Tomas is getting worried that his concerns about money aren't being heard. They are both relying on different approaches to deal with their growing feelings. Sarah is getting angrier, louder and a bit sarcastic. Tomas, on the other hand, is turning to logic and seemingly rational arguments, and 'what it's normal for people to do'. This seems to have an impact on Sarah – is the implication that she isn't normal? And it perhaps gives a sense that her opinion isn't valued. As their emotions start to run higher, these override any capacity to have a productive conversation and it feels as if this is a conversation that isn't going to help them work out any kind of satisfactory solution.

Getting this wrong with each other may be an inevitable stepping stone on their path of learning to communicate better. If they can see this conversation as getting them to a place that doesn't work for them, they can then take the view that there may be a different way that's going to be more effective. They need to find a way to listen to each other differently.

Contrast:

SARAH: I really don't want to live an hour away from work even if it does mean we can save a bit more.
TOMAS: Yeah, I know, you keep saying that. What's that about do you think?

Now, even though Tomas may have his own set of feelings about the situation, he has acknowledged Sarah's feelings, is being curious about them and is giving her a space to describe them. This changes the whole shape of the conversation that follows.

SARAH: I just feel like it's hard enough to get organised in the mornings already; let alone doing it with half the time.

TOMAS: Yes – I know that is your least favourite thing.

Tomas has shown that he has heard what she said. She might feel she has been listened to. He is managing to wait for a chance to air his own feelings and his view of how things should be.

SARAH: It would be nice to have a bit more space though, and I know money is on your mind.

Because Sarah feels listened to by Tomas, and her thoughts have been given space, she feels it's safer to explore the other side of the argument, to explore his views. Even if Tomas doesn't agree with her concerns, he hasn't diminished them (or her sense of herself) by saying that normal people wouldn't have those concerns or by trying to talk her out of her feelings. Because of this she doesn't have to hold on to such an extreme position any more. She experiences her concerns as having been noticed and this means that she doesn't need to turn the volume up to try to be heard.

TOMAS: Yeah, it would make a big difference, I think that's what I'm really thinking about.

SARAH: Oh I don't know, it's so hard deciding, how are we going to manage it! I guess we should start looking and see how we feel about it all.

This now has the feel of a shared project in which they are both involved, rather than one in which they are obstructing or thwarting each other.

TOMAS: Good plan. I'm sure we'll figure it out.

Although the conversation starts in the same way, this time Tomas's capacity to acknowledge Sarah's position by saying 'Yeah, I know, you keep saying that' radically changes the course of the conversation (even though her concerns are different from his). Instead of being caught up in a defensive conversation, they can feel a bit more optimistic and collaborative.

Acknowledgement is such an underrated friend but it can be so helpful. If you are able to acknowledge what your partner has said (which doesn't mean that you're agreeing with their ideas) then that creates a link between you. It shows that you have heard what your partner has to say. Sometimes we worry that if we acknowledge what our partner is feeling then it means that their feeling 'wins' or becomes more important.

Tomas might at some level, conscious or not, feel that if he gives space to Sarah's worries about living an hour away then perhaps her ideas will win the day. Instead, the opposite seems to happen. In feeling that her view and her feelings have been acknowledged, Sarah can relax a bit and be more interested in Tomas's ideas too. They seem to be creating a dynamic in which there is enough room for both of their ideas to be heard, rather than it being a battle for one set of ideas. This doesn't take away the need for them to decide what they are going to do, and there will still be compromises between them, but they are giving themselves a better setting, or framework, in which to make that decision, simply by clarifying that they've heard each other.

Tomas also opens up the conversation with his question 'What's that about?' He is curious about Sarah and that seems to mean a lot to her. It's not always easy to be curious. Sometimes we are so caught up in our own feelings or our own wish to get our point across that we can forget to be curious. Or so worried that we won't be listened to that this becomes all we think about. We are waiting for the other person to finish speaking so that we can start. When we can listen only for the purpose of trying to comprehend each other it can be a total game-changer.

Good curious openers
- *What do you think that's about?*
- *What do you mean?*
- *Can you help me understand that?*
- *Would it help to talk about this?*

Thinking about small details can change the big picture. The acknowledgement and curiosity in the second conversation create a more relaxed exchange. If you don't feel heard, it makes sense to try to speak more loudly or more angrily or by bringing in evidence or rational arguments. You might feel that you have to express your feelings more vehemently – which is how things can get polarised. One minute you're mulling around some ideas with your partner and the next, when you start to feel they're not hearing you, you're nailing your colours to the mast and your partner is nailing their colours to the mast and it's not even clear that you had those colours in the first place, or at least in the technicolour in which they now appear. Sometimes this relates to experiences we've had over and over again in our histories, where we haven't been listened to by the people close to us. This can make us particularly sensitive to people expressing different ideas to ours and particularly worried that there won't be room for us to put our point of view.

If, on the other hand, you feel heard, as Sarah does in the second conversation, there's more room for mixed feelings to emerge – 'Oh I don't know, it's so hard deciding'. Their conversation becomes much less of a 'my way or your way' conversation and much more about trying to figure it out together rather than each of them trying to impose their vision on the other.

This also means that they can capitalise on each other's ideas and styles. Sarah is taking care of one aspect in their life: how rushed they are going to feel, how stressed they might get if they have less time; Tomas is taking care of the financial side of things. If they can each move away from feeling that they need to fight to be heard, they can make better use of the other's different – and potentially complementary – resources. What is happening is that they are creating a more robust setting for thinking about things, because they aren't thrown off course by the other having a different idea.

This shift from having conversations in an unproductive as opposed to a productive way will be an important transition for them as a couple in terms of better communicating. It is in that sense an argument they need to have.

Ideas for reflection

- *How easy is it for you to listen to someone? Next time you are in a conversation, tune into how you are listening to the other person. Notice – do you interrupt, do you feel like you need to say your side of things, are you listening to understand them or with a thought in your mind about what you want to say next? Do you stay with the thing they are telling you, or do you move on to a different subject?*
- *Generally, are you optimistic that you will get listened to by other people?*
- *How do you feel you were listened to in your family?*

Why do you feel you need to fix everything!

The importance of acknowledgement and curiosity comes up in another conversation between Sarah and Tomas and is one that I see often with couples when they have different approaches to dealing with each other's upset or difficult feelings. Tomas's style is to be a problem-solver. When Sarah is struggling with something, he wants to offer her practical solutions. Indeed, this is a skill he has at work. However, Sarah isn't so keen on this approach. When Tomas offers her a solution, it might make her feel as if he isn't listening to her or perhaps can't manage what is being said – or perhaps that she is inadequate in some way.

Tomas is the complete opposite. When he is upset, he would prefer Sarah to give him advice or a solution. Instead, she seems to him to want to talk about his problem at greater length, when he just wants to move on and think about something else. They both tend to offer each other the response they would like for themselves rather than the one geared to the other.

TOMAS: How was your day?

SARAH: Bad actually ... I couldn't stop worrying about where we are going to move to and how it's going to work and I was a bit distracted.

TOMAS: Oh no! You shouldn't let it get into your work day.

SARAH: Yeah but I just kept thinking about it and imagining what it would be like doing the commute.

TOMAS: You know what, you should promise yourself that you'll only think about it when you get home – there's nothing you can do about it at work anyway.

SARAH: That's not the point. Anyway, it doesn't matter, I sort of feel like you don't get it.

So Tomas has his idea of how to help her but in fact from her point of view, he doesn't 'get it'. And what Sarah doesn't 'get' is that it's because he cares that he is trying to offer her a solution. She feels that in telling her how to deal with it differently he is closing down the space she needs to talk about it. They are coming at this conversation with good intentions but with completely different mindsets and they need to find a way to manage this. If they can be more aware of these aspects of each other then they will be able to offer a response that is more tailored to what each of them is like and more understanding of the ways in which they might get it wrong with one another.

Knowing these things about one's partner is a constant

work in progress. I think a helpful question to keep in mind is 'what do you need?' This brings the conversation back to something simple, a space where both people can talk about what they might need. It doesn't mean that there will be an easy answer, but at least if needs are known they can be considered.

SARAH: That's not the point. Anyway, it doesn't matter, I sort of feel like you don't get it.

TOMAS: Okay – I seem to not be getting it. I do want to get it. What would help? What do you need here?

SARAH: Nothing really – just for you to register that I'm finding this all hard and to be able to tell you about it.

TOMAS: I do know that you find it really hard; I think sometimes you think that I forget that.

SARAH: I don't think that, it's just that for me sometimes I need to say things again; it helps me to be able to say it out loud to you; and I need you to know that you don't need to come up with an answer for me when I'm talking about a problem.

TOMAS: It's hard – that's just what I'm like ... I hope you can see I'm only trying to help.

SARAH: It helps me to be reminded of that. I think I just need to know that you know that this is what works for me when I am feeling upset about something. I'm sure I get it wrong with you sometimes and perhaps there's a way you'd like me to be helpful to you when you are feeling upset?

TOMAS: One of the things I like you to do when I'm upset is when you break down the problem for me.

You're really good at seeing what needs to be done to sort something out.

There is something dynamic here – they are having to work hard at making themselves understood rather than expecting each other to get it right first time. By asking 'what do you need?' Tomas creates a space for Sarah to convey what she is feeling. It also creates a space in which each of them can clarify things with the other about how to respond when they are feeling upset about something. They've given up an idea that they will instinctively know what the other one needs, and they are now working hard to actually find out what it is – which they may also need to work out for themselves too.

This dynamic can also come up when couples are talking not about problems external to their relationship (as in Sarah's bad day) but also in problems within their relationship. A 'problem-solver' may feel that if their partner is complaining about something that has happened between them in the past, then nothing they can do will change it and therefore the only solution may be to offer an apology. This may help – but the partner who isn't a problem-solver may need the experience of knowing that their partner has heard their complaint (and needs to process it by talking about it). They may not need a solution – more to know that by talking about it they are being engaged with. It can be baffling for someone who wouldn't talk more than once about something in the past to hear their partner talking about it over and over again, but this may indicate that their partner feels they aren't being listened to.

Ideas for reflection
- *If you have a problem, what makes you feel better? A concrete solution or being able to talk about it? Or both?*
- *What do you know about your partner in this area?*
- *What does your partner know about you in this area?*

You just don't get it!
Tomas is upset and cross that Sarah ate on her way home from the gym without telling him. He had gone out to the shops to get dinner and had made it for them both.

TOMAS: That's so thoughtless of you. It would have been helpful if you could have let me know.

SARAH: Sorry, I was just so hungry after my class – it doesn't have to be a big deal, does it?

TOMAS: Well, next time can you tell me?

SARAH: How about next time you tell me that you are planning to make a big deal out of dinner?

Both of them feel that the other one could have communicated better. In making the shift to being in a couple, their communication needs to be upgraded to take the other one into account. One of the huge and disappointing realities we have to face about our partners is that they aren't mind readers; they don't think in the same way we do, don't know about the things that might upset us, and don't respond to what we've said in the way we assume they will. Having to bridge the gap with words can often feel like a poor substitution.

This need to spell things out to our partners – things

that seem completely obvious to us – can feel like hard work. Often couples bring rows to therapy in the hopes that their partner will learn to read their minds better, or that I will teach them a magic way of communicating with each other. Instead, the outcome is more often a coming to terms with the fact that they need to spell things out more clearly. When two individuals each have a different first language, making meaning clear may need particular effort, but even if a couple share a primary language, work will still be needed on an ongoing basis to keep clarifying things to one another.

We can also get into situations where we 'set ourselves up' for communication failure (even if we don't realise we are doing it). Sometimes the longing to be understood and to have our minds read means that we really don't want to have to spell it out; or we just forget to – and yet when our partner then gets it wrong we feel really disappointed, without them even understanding why what they've done is disappointing. If we can accept this understandable response, even if it's a bit disillusioning, then we can be more compassionate with one another when we (inevitably) get our wires crossed.

I feel like I'm banging my head against a brick wall

Couples often tell me that there are issues that they have tried to bring up with each other for years, or over and over again, but that they feel they're banging their head against a brick wall. It is often after years of this feeling that one half of a couple walks in to tell me that their relationship is over. The feeling of being on the wrong side of the brick wall or door or whatever leaves them feeling alone, unheard, and sometimes desperate. Sometimes it seems that both feel that they're on the wrong side of a brick wall, with their thoughts never quite reaching the other side.

Part of my job with couples is to try to establish what those brick walls are for. Although the barrier can seem angry or rigid or mean, it may be that there's something behind it that needs protecting – which is why the wall gets put up in the first place. A more vulnerable feeling, perhaps, or something more fragile or anxious. When our partner says something about us or when they touch on a sore point, we may want to protect ourselves by being defensive or trying to make them feel similarly hurt. If the comment they make resonates with a difficult experience from the past, it may feel even more important to put up those defences. Similarly, if we say something to our partners that is hurtful to them (even if we didn't know it), we may get this brick wall response.

Josh and Ryan are a couple with two children. Ryan works freelance with his own hours, and he has the main childcaring role between them, whereas Josh works long hours and often has to work late because of time differences with his American office. Ryan picks the kids up from school. Josh often comes home so that he can see the children but then carries on working on his phone. Ryan hates the situation. He hates that Josh is there physically, but because he is preoccupied with work, he is not really there emotionally for the family. Whenever he tries to talk about it with Josh the conversation turns very spiky and ends up with Josh saying, 'What do you want me to do, quit my job?' Ryan really feels he is on the wrong side of a brick wall here.

Ryan is trying to bring it up again, even though he feels he will meet the same response as always:

RYAN: Why can't you just stay in the office late two days a week rather than come home and be around but not available? You just don't think of us.

JOSH: It's not like I have any control in this. I can't believe you are still going on about this. Are we seriously going to have this conversation again?!

RYAN: You just create such a bad atmosphere when you're around. The kids need to come home and relax and there you are on the phone and you don't see how frustrated they get about it? You also set such a bad example by being on the phone all the time.

JOSH: You have no idea. Seriously. I am not going to talk about this with you. If you only knew the pressure I'm under at the moment at work. What planet are you on?

This exchange is getting them nowhere. Josh defends himself from Ryan's criticism by criticising him back and by refusing to take his position on board. Ryan feels yet again that Josh has ducked the issue and this obstructs them ever having a conversation about the situation. He feels that Josh is completely insensitive and rude.

There are lots of painful aspects to this state of affairs that might need protecting with brick walls. Josh may feel conflicted about being unable to be present for the children. Perhaps it touches a nerve for him – it may depend on his own experience of how he was parented.

Ryan may feel alone in his childcaring role and perhaps envious that Josh doesn't have that responsibility. There are painful realities about having to go out to work, which intrudes on family life, and the fact that one of them gets to spend more time with the children than the other.

However, none of these painful aspects has a safe place to be revealed at the moment because they are hidden behind the brick walls of their defensive comments to each other. Is there a way in which they could soften the conversation so that the brick walls don't need to be built so high or so quickly? A different way might be:

RYAN: Look, I know you hate me bringing this up, but I'm really struggling with your work at the moment – and I know you probably are too. I find it so hard that you are around but not available.

JOSH: Yes, it's awful. I hate it but I don't know what to do, I want to be with the kids before they go to bed but then I can't find any other way to get the work done.

RYAN: I'm not sure I can go on with it like this.

JOSH: I don't know what to do but we really need to have a think about working things out differently.

In this example, because Ryan is able to speak about feeling bad, rather than starting off by accusing Josh and making him feel bad, the conversation has the chance to be more productive. Ryan isn't attributing the whole situation to Josh. This leaves room for Josh to feel that he isn't completely under attack from Ryan, so he doesn't need to be so defensive and doesn't need to protect himself so much. They seem to generate, between them, a capacity for thinking, and seem to be more sympathetic to their relationship as they share in the disappointment and painfulness of the situation. Rather than criticising each other, they are looking at the relationship from the outside and acknowledging that it's in a difficult place.

Ryan can also help Josh with the more difficult feelings he has about missing out on being at home.

> RYAN: Is there any way that you think it would be easier on all of us, you included, if you stayed later at the office one or two nights a week? I know that is really sad for you but in some ways I think it might be more efficient and then we aren't winding each other up in front of the children and then perhaps on the days you are home you can finish earlier.

Josh looks sad and Ryan comforts him. There is some capacity here to be sad together about the situation rather than angry about it, and it seems as if they may be able to make a plan that is more workable. Even though it may mean Josh having to give something up, this is more manageable now that they are working on it together.

Ryan starting off by talking about what he feels is so important. Couples say things to me such as 'When we know how the other one is feeling, it makes it so much easier to care for each other. If we are just being blamed by the other, then we don't really feel like responding or caring.' This change in dynamic from blame to speaking in terms of how we ourselves are feeling can create more productive conversations.

This is why sentences that start with 'I' help. An 'I' sentence may be more likely to invite help from the other person rather than put their back up. Sentences that start with 'it' also help. 'It' is a small but helpful word as it can be used to describe a shared situation rather than point the finger. 'It seems difficult for us to talk about this' might be a more helpful way into a conversation than 'you're always so rubbish at listening'. It helps flag up that this is a relationship problem that you can both start to think about, rather than a problem that lies with just one of you.

It's natural that when we have an uncomfortable feeling we want to blame it on someone else, or find another place to put it. Ryan is feeling a bit alone in the situation. But ironically, when he blames Josh for the situation he gets a reaction that is likely to leave him more alone. If he can name or attempt to describe his more vulnerable feeling, it seems that he will be more likely to get some help with it.

These uncomfortable feelings may be so deep down that we aren't even aware of them ourselves, relating perhaps to old experiences that are painful and sensitive. More delicate feelings may often get hidden behind brick walls. Sometimes a safe therapy setting is where they can be made known and tended to. If we can develop a curious mindset (back to the importance of curiosity) it can allow room for these more delicate feelings to be exposed. It's unrealistic to think that brick walls can be completely demolished; more realistic is to think of how to create ways through, how to help each other not have such high or thick walls. And we can also learn something about our partners from noticing where their brick walls seem to be. When we have an argument with our partner, or feel as if we are confronting something defensive, perhaps this is a moment to pause and think – is there more to understand here about why this is causing such a reaction? Because if we can start to understand what it is that's so painful for them then we have an opportunity to learn something really important. Similarly, when something they say or do is really painful for us, it can flag up something that we may need to think about in ourselves; when our partner hits a nerve, maybe they are on to something that needs some attention. Being in a couple gives us the opportunity to be in the smallest kind of group therapy – if we can work at finding a safe way to talk about difficult things with each other, then we also have an opportunity to develop. These difficult feelings may then start to feel less dangerous and frightening as we know more about them and reduce our need to defend against them.

Ideas for reflection
- *How do you tend to bring things up with your partner? For example, about how you are feeling or how you think they have behaved?*
- *Are you able to reframe a criticism of your partner into a sentence that starts I not You?*
- *How do you respond if your partner brings up something that they are struggling with?*

You always sound so critical!

When it comes to communicating, tone has a huge impact. It's not necessarily the words we choose or the way we describe our feelings that can cause upset, but simply the tone in which we say them. When couples engage more fully with how they hear one another's tone, this can help to shift a conversation from being one that brings out the worst in them (one that will put someone's back up) to one that is productive. For example, some people are more sensitive to a critical tone than others, which may relate to experiences they have had of people being critical, authoritative or unpleasant.

Having a conversation together about this seems to be helpful: that is, being curious about how you hear each other's tone, and giving each other space to describe what tone can mean to you. We can also use tone as information. If we constantly hear our partners talking in an angry tone (or even washing up in an angry tone) then perhaps there is something more important that needs dealing with. Perhaps it isn't the most straightforward way to express feelings to each other, but sometimes our tone is one step ahead of our capacity to express our feelings. Can you both use the feel of the tone as a warning sign that you need to sit down together and have a chat? It may be uncomfortable to engage with it, but if you or your partner always sounds angry is this a sign that something needs addressing?

Ideas for reflection
- *Do you care about the tone in which something is said to you? Do you feel sensitive to it? What impact does your*

partner's tone have on you? Does it remind you of other people's tones?

- *How do you think your tone comes across?*

Why do you always go from 0 to 60?

One of the problems frequently raised is where one person in the couple says that they hate the way their partner 'goes from 0 to 60'. They feel that their partner suddenly gets angry out of the blue, and to them this seems disproportionate, unjustified and often shocking or unpleasant. They may end up arguing, not about anything substantive but actually about the anger being expressed – a 'why are you behaving so disproportionately here' type of argument that is preoccupied with the idea that one person is overreacting.

If this anger is unsafe or threatening then clearly it needs to be taken seriously. (More about this towards the end of the chapter – see the paragraph 'keeping safe' and also Appendix 2). If it were safe to do so, where there were arguments like this, I'd be thinking with a couple about different aspects of their dynamic such as:

- What is the impact of the angry expression on the person facing it?
- What is the anger really about?
- Has the person who is expressing their anger actually been angry for a while – and could they have flagged this up earlier? (And if not, what was difficult about that?)
- Or has the person on the end of the angry

outburst missed opportunities for understanding earlier on?

- Is there anything the 'non-angry' person is angry about but finds it hard to express openly?

Reflecting on these kinds of questions may help a couple attend to an issue before it needs to come out explosively and may help them to see it in terms of a dynamic between them rather than a problem with just one of them.

What's with the silent treatment?

Caz and Damian, a couple in their twenties, gave me a taste of the way they communicated from the first moment they sat down in my consulting room. Caz sat down and turned her back to Damian, her arms crossed, not really talking. When I asked her why she thought they were here for help, she said that I should ask Damian – 'He's the one who thinks we have problems'. She was clearly in a huge sulk with him and didn't want to discuss anything.

Damian looked at me and said, 'You see? This is what I have to deal with. And then you wonder why we are here?' He seemed to think Caz was the problem, and Caz, with all her body, seemed to be saying that Damian was.

It wasn't that this couple weren't communicating. They were communicating very powerfully. Without knowing what it was all about, I was curious to find out more. I had a sense that under Caz's sulk there was something vulnerable and upset, but it was being covered up by this hard shell of a sulk which filled the atmosphere in the room. The silence of the sulk was so powerful it distracted us from any opportunity to think about what was going on. It was clear that Damian was meant to know what she was feeling.

A bit like the 'o to 60' type couple, where the attention gets diverted to the angry outburst, here the attention was being diverted to the sulky behaviour rather than what might be underneath it. Clearly there were some strong feelings around that we needed to understand better. In order to make any progress, each of them were going to have to give up the positions they were holding. Caz would have to give up an idea that Damian could mind-read and Damian would have to get beyond the sulk and try to help create a space for understanding what was going on, by listening. When they could step back and see that something was going on between them, that the sulk was a sign of something more vulnerable that needed understanding and tending to, it became possible for them to begin a more useful conversation about why Caz was actually upset.

It also became possible for Damian to say something about the impact Caz's sulking had on him. 'When Caz gets sulky, it does have an impact on me. It actually upsets me quite a bit, and I feel a bit panicked by it. It's horrible, in fact. I feel like whatever I say is going to go wrong. It's not nice being on eggshells.'

It was a bit of a surprise to Caz to hear about the impact of her sulking on Damian. She said that often she got so caught up in her upset that she didn't think so much about how it might feel for him. She said it was hard, that this was her default when she felt angry, and that it was a way of not saying things she didn't want to say. It was a way of not blurting things out that might seem rude. When they could talk about these sulking episodes while not in the middle of them, it seemed as if they could be more compassionate with each other about the dynamic they got into and also be more aware of how not to get into it. Caz said 'I guess I have to give up on my hope that he'll magically know why I am upset with him.' Damian said 'I do want to know what's going on. Even if I don't like hearing it, it's important that you tell me – I'd much rather that than just get a cold shoulder because honestly I'm not very good at decoding cold shoulders.'

Neither of them much liked the sulking episodes, but they realised that if they wanted to avoid them they were perhaps going to need to work a bit harder at conversations in which their feelings could be described and listened to.

Ideas for reflection
- *Is sulking a theme in your relationship?*
- *What works for you if you are feeling in a sulk? Do you want to be talked to or left alone? Does it help if you're left alone but that that is acknowledged between you, i.e. 'I can see you're cross and don't want to talk but I'm here if you need me.'*
- *What does it feel like if you are on the end of a sulk?*

We hate conflict (or avoid it)
Clearly if a couple are functioning and getting on well without conflict and this works for them, then fine – as the saying goes, 'if it ain't broke don't fix it'. But there

are couples I've worked with who do whatever they can (however aware they are of this) to avoid any difficult conversations. The risk of this is the elephant-in-the-room factor. If issues that they feel differently about or cross or resentful about don't get tended to occasionally, then sometimes couples find themselves in crisis because there is an elephant in the room that has grown so big that there's no space left to move. When couples in crisis like this come for help they often wish they had come earlier – about 'two or three years ago' – but clearly they didn't, and that was perhaps because it would have been so frightening to do so.

Sometimes the elephant has grown so big that there is no room left for the relationship. Or they have a herd of various elephants that both are invested in looking after, perhaps without realising it.

Ruth was in her early fifties. She sought help on her own in therapy as she was ending her marriage to her husband Ray because of their 'communication issues'. They had been together for twenty-five years and had two teenage children. She said that she had realised that she was longing for something more intimate but that Ray was very 'unemotional', 'very bad at talking', and 'never interested in how she felt'.

She felt they had become two co-parents, rather than a couple, and said that their sex life was non-existent. She felt overburdened in the relationship, angry with Ray that she dealt with the children and the house far more than she felt he did, and unacknowledged in her role. She was angry with him too that he was 'hopeless with money'. She had emailed him to tell him their marriage was over.

Some of the issues she faced are issues I will look at in other chapters later in the book. How had Ruth ended up in a role she felt resentful about? What had happened to their sex life? But what Ruth kept coming back to was the poor quality of communication in their relationship. They hadn't found a way between them to address issues that she had been unhappy about for years and which now seemed beyond repair. She said that they both avoided conflict but it seemed that doing so had led to a complete breakdown of intimacy between them.

Ruth put it all in terms of Ray being the one who was 'bad at talking', but I wondered with her if there was a part of her that had avoided it too. If we could think about it in terms of what might have happened between them, something that perhaps they had both been a part of, we could learn something about what hadn't been possible. It seemed that they hadn't found a language between them to deal with any of these issues. If perhaps they had occasionally been angry with each other, or found a way to communicate their upset, they might have learned more about each other even if that had meant conflict. Instead, they seemed to have moved further and further away from each other. Ruth described a feeling that they were on parallel tracks, never converging about anything. She sought therapy on her own – perhaps the thought of both of them being there was just too much.

The reasons behind a couple like Ruth and Ray not being able to communicate are deep and complex. It isn't about flicking a switch and saying 'start talking'. Fears about opening up to someone, fears about what saying something controversial might risk, can relate to deeply held experiences that may be based on a style of communicating that someone has grown up with. In Ruth's case she said that the 'rug in her house was a foot high, there were so many things swept under it'. It emerged that her father had been an unhappy man and her mother had had an affair. Everyone knew about it but it was never mentioned. She wondered now if her father had been suffering from depression.

What had made Ruth seek help now was that her teenage daughter was struggling with anxiety at school and had been referred to the school counsellor. The counsellor had reported back to Ruth that she was hearing that there seemed to be a tense atmosphere at home. This was hard for Ruth to hear. It was painful for her to think that she and her husband had created an atmosphere like that. She said she tried hard to bury her head in the sand about her relationship but now that her daughter was finding it hard she realised it couldn't go on. She didn't want her daughter to grow up and think that this was a healthy way to have a relationship. She realised that she and her husband were repeating the model her parents had given her of how to communicate.

We all bring our unique experiences to the way we communicate with our partner: the way we have been listened to or spoken to (or not); the language that has been used with us; the different 'norms' we inherit of how we communicate; what we feel about conflict; and even what our idea of funny is (or is not). What seems normal to us may be very different from that of our partner, and it can be a game-changer to increase our awareness of what these 'norms' are.

I'll say more about family in the next chapter, but mapping our different experiences of communication can be a useful starting point when thinking about difficulties in this area. It's something I often ask couples in the early days of meeting them – how did you talk about things in your families? Did that work for you? What idea do you have about how couples work things out between them?

The risk for a couple in failing to find a way of talking about the difficult things is that it can build up, as it did in this situation with Ruth. If there is a tendency towards avoiding talking about difficult stuff, a pull of old that comes from the way in which it was done in your family, it can be helpful to become more aware of this.

Ideas for reflection
- *What model do you have from your upbringing of how to talk about difficult things?*
- *What are the channels in your relationship like for talking about something difficult?*

You don't understand me!
These differences in communication styles don't always need to be thought about in the context of family backgrounds. Another thing that couples find helpful is to consider how they are wired differently, or have different operating systems or different capacities. If we all came into our relationships with an instruction manual I'd probably be out of a job, because so much of my work is about creating a space in which couples can get to know the other better. Being in a relationship involves getting to know each other better, of knowing which buttons to

push (or not). The more self-awareness someone has, the easier it will be to explain to the other person how to get the best out of them when it comes to communicating (and which buttons not to press). Equally, the process of being in a relationship can be a way of getting to know yourself better as you discover which things you find easy or difficult.

For example, one of you might like to work out what you think about something by talking openly about it, whereas the other might feel they can only talk about something once they know what they think about it. One may be a planner, who likes to schedule a time to talk about something, and one of you might be more spontaneous. One might need no distractions to be able to focus on a conversation or one might feel more comfortable with having a chat on a walk or while driving. One of you might be more distractible than the other and find it harder to settle into a conversation about one topic. One of you may feel overloaded more quickly than the other by information from the other person. One might respond differently to shouting than the other. One of you may have less good hearing and need a better setting to actually be able to hear what is being said.

Some differences or difficulties in communicating may be understood and accepted more easily by understanding more about neurodiversity and how different people's brains work differently. Where there is curiosity and understanding and a willingness to accept that we all have our different starting points when it comes to communicating, couples can then start to tailor their conversations better to match each other's sensitivities.

Communication

Annie and Lena always got into a particular pattern when they tried to talk about something difficult. Annie would bring something controversial up out of the blue and Lena, in Annie's view, would get upset very quickly and it would become impossible to have a conversation. Lena would storm off, which Annie would find very upsetting, and then the argument would not be about the issue Annie was trying to bring up but about the way the argument had gone.

Even when we recognise a dynamic in our relationships that's difficult, it's hard to change it. Annie could continue to bring up controversial matters in this way in their relationship, hoping that this time it would work, and could keep on getting the same reaction. Similarly, Lena could keep on storming off and upsetting Annie. This isn't to say that anyone is particularly to blame for the situation, it's just that the way they are doing things doesn't seem to bring out the best in the conversation. But if couples don't do the hard work of thinking about how to change dynamics then it's hard to envisage how they can change. What Annie and Lena might need to give up here is the idea that doing the same thing is going to get a different reaction.

A helpful conversation between them might reflect on the situation in a bit more detail. Lena might become aware that she sometimes needs more time than Annie to process something, that storming off has become her way of coping with difficult feelings. If she could explain this to Annie (not in the heat of the moment) and Annie could take it on board, then maybe Annie could go more slowly on difficult issues and this would help them both find the necessary forum in which to discuss things. It could also give Annie a chance to convey to Lena what the storming off means to her.

Noticing the different styles and capacities we have for talking about difficult things requires fine tuning, not only in respect of the other but also in ourselves. By getting a handle on these differences (which we are probably going to discover by getting them wrong) we can attempt to have more productive conversations with each other. Even if it doesn't always look neat, at least it gives a difficult conversation its best chance.

> ### Idea for reflection
> - *What setting or style of talking helps a conversation go well for you?*

You always bring things up at the worst time

I worked in a programme during lockdown to help couples seeking support on how to manage their relationship better at this time. One of the themes that came up again and again was the timing of conversations between them. With no boundaries between home and work, couples felt that they had different ideas about good times and bad times for conversations.

Peter and Esther sought help as they felt that they kept arguing about this. They said that the point at which Peter came home from work had always been a fractious one for them. Esther, after a long day at home with their toddler and older children, would want to tell him about her day, but Peter would often want to go and unwind before he could engage with the family.

In lockdown he found this even harder – his commute home was 'down the stairs into the kitchen'. He felt that as soon as he came out of the room upstairs where he was working from home, Esther wanted to speak to him about things. He said he found it hard. He knew it was hard for Esther too and that she was desperate to talk after a long and fretful day of childcare and home-schooling. Together we thought about the reality of this and about how to focus more on making a suitable time to speak to each other once the children were in bed. Esther said that it meant hanging on to her feelings for longer and that sometimes that was hard, but if he was more receptive then it was probably worth it.

Lockdown or not, thinking about the timing of conversations is crucial for couples. Life is busy, and it isn't always a good time to talk. Keeping the communication flowing between you keeps you in touch with each other but at the same time it isn't possible to deal with everyone's feelings all of the time. It can be hard to hold on to intense feelings about something when you want to express them, but it may not be the best moment for either you or your partner, whether because one of you isn't in the right frame of mind or you're about to go to sleep or you're having to deal with something else at that point. I have worked with a lot of sleep-deprived parents over the years and always think with them about whether today is a helpful day to address something controversial or hard – are they in a good frame of mind? There is inevitably going to be a learning-from-mistakes quality to figuring out what works for you both in terms of timing.

There's also a very serious point about timing where

children are concerned if you are having a difficult conversation or getting into something troubling. This issue really needs consideration, because it is not healthy for your children to witness or be exposed to an escalation of conflict between you. This isn't easy – parents have more things to argue about and less time in which to do so (more of this in chapter 6). This doesn't mean you can't disagree with your partner in front of your children, and it can be positive if you can model to your children how you can have different opinions on something and find a way through them. But as I keep coming back to, frequent, poor and unresolved conflict is harmful for children and being able to keep thinking about what the children might be experiencing is crucial. If a couple don't have a capacity to think about the timing of conversations in this way, and can't agree on a safety mechanism to stop difficult or escalating conversations or arguments before they ramp up too much, then this is a sign that help may be needed.

Ideas for reflection
- *What time and space do you make to talk about things that are on your mind?*
- *Is there a time that works well for you to check in with each other? Is that something you could actively plan?*
- *What times don't work well to talk?*
- *Is it okay for one of you to say, 'Now is not a good time?'*

Picking your battles
Picking battles sounds like a good idea but is easier said than done. How can couples go about making better decisions about the arguments they do and don't need to

have? This links in very much with the ideas above about timing. Picking battles can often mean picking the timing of battles.

I hope that some of the ideas in this book will help couples to tend better to the issues between them so that they don't leak into all conversations or areas between them and they don't need to communicate their frustrations through all mediums possible, including the washing-up. When someone feels 'my partner is on at me about everything' this may be a sign that there's something deeper that needs attention, and if that issue can be tended to then it will be easier to drop some of the 'battles'.

There is also a reflectiveness that is required in order to pick battles:

- Is this a road we've been down before?
- Are we heading down it in the same way as always?
- If so, is there any point having it or is it time to try to think about it in a different way?
- Can I live without making this point today, here and now?
- Maybe it is driving me crazy that you've left your shoes on the floor again, but is it really worth bringing it up?
- How do I think this is going to go if I do bring it up right here right now?

I'm very much not advising that you sweep things under the carpet for an easier life but sometimes it's worth taking a breath before launching into a complaint and thinking – is now the right moment for this? Is this really likely to bring about the outcome I want or is there a better or more productive way in which I can deal with this?

Sometimes there won't be, which is why it is important that we have repairing conversations ...

Repairing conversations

Developing a capacity to think together about your disagreements or arguments after the event is maybe one of the most important things on which a couple can work. Indeed, a lot of my work with couples is just that – it's in the thinking about the places where couples disagree that we learn the most about what matters to them. These repairing conversations literally have the capacity to re-pair, to get you back into 'pair' mode. Or another way of putting it would be that it's how you get the relationship back on track after a disagreement has derailed things. And it's not just getting it back on track – what's really important is to think of these moments as offering an important opportunity to learn something about each other and ourselves. Every time we are out of tune with our partner and they let us know about it, there's an opportunity to tune in to them better. Every time our partner makes a painful complaint about us there's an opportunity to tune in to what their experience of us might be. There is a 'stitch in time' element here. If we don't work at repairing things when we get out of tune with each other, even the small things, then we can get disconnected from each other and issues can build up.

People often tell me that there's an argument that they

have again and again and again. Whether it's a row on the way home from the in-laws or the argument about the towels left on the bed or the coming back home too late again, there's something about these repeated arguments that couples feel they can't get away from and don't know how to improve.

One way of dealing with these repeated arguments is to do nothing, to keep having the same argument again and again. For some couples these repeated arguments are old slippers that feel a familiar part of their relationship, a way of defining themselves or visiting difficult issues that the couple can live with without resolving. But some repetitive arguments cause distress every time. The argument that crops up is a flawed attempt at resolving the issues.

One way to convert the argument into something more useful is to make time when emotions are not high and to think about it in the cool of the moment; to actively try to observe together what was going on and what each of you understood about where the other one was coming from – to think and be curious about what it was that they were trying to convey so emotively.

This does of course risk opening up the row again, and is often why people avoid doing it. Agreeing some rules in advance can help with this. For example, 'if we start to feel upset as we discuss it, let's wait until we cool down'. If it always feels too raw or too sensitive an issue to discuss together then maybe it's a sign that you could do with some help from a third party to think about the issue safely together.

It's in this repair job that we get to learn about each other.

Things can be clarified and reclarified. Communicating well is a messy process of visiting and revisiting issues. It takes time for us, let alone for our partners, to understand why we feel strongly about something.

Jackson and Naomi had had an argument because Jackson had said that Naomi's family were being too intrusive and critical of his choice to resign from his job and start his own business. Naomi felt very protective of her family and it made her quite defensive; Jackson felt really angry and said some quite critical things about them. They had had this argument before.

JACKSON: I'm sorry we argued last night.

NAOMI: I still can't believe you said the things you did about my family. I didn't know you felt like that.

JACKSON: Look, I've said sorry, what more do you want?

NAOMI: I don't see how that can be the end of it.

JACKSON: I don't know what to say if you won't accept my apology. Isn't that enough?

This conversation about the argument doesn't really get them anywhere. Jackson's sorry is a bit of a roadblock and there isn't any capacity to learn about the situation. The 'sorry' doesn't really take them anywhere.

Contrast:

JACKSON: I'm sorry we argued last night.

NAOMI: I still can't believe that you said the things you did about my family. I didn't know you felt like that.

JACKSON: Look, I know I said some cruel things but I find this really upsetting. When your dad criticised my decision, it really hit a nerve; I know your dad is worried but I guess I am a bit worried too.

Jackson describes his own upset – which seems to make it easier for Naomi to get in touch with some sympathy for him as well as with her own feelings.

NAOMI: I know. I'm sorry. He can be so blunt sometimes. I'm upset too. It was hurtful hearing what you said about him.
JACKSON: I know. I went too far but it was in the heat of the moment. I know it's only that they're worried about us …
NAOMI: Well, okay. But tell me what is it that you're worried about?

This is a much more honest and curious conversation – it's perhaps painful and risky to own some of their fears and worries, but they are now sharing in a dialogue and will feel much more supported by one another. Rather than there being a roadblock to learning from their argument, they've gone on a detour that might actually help them learn something about each other, which in turn may help them get back on the 'main road' and make them feel closer. Understanding what the nerve is that Jackson feels has been 'hit' may be really important.

Why can't you just say sorry!
What's also constructive here is how Jackson and Naomi

both own their part in the argument, both of them using the word sorry. It's brave to do that, as it risks the other person saying 'yes, it is all your fault', but it also opens up a possibility for the other person to do the same, to speak to their part. If there is a general climate of communication within a couple that seeks to encourage listening and to make it safe to speak about difficult feelings then this makes the climate in which to say sorry much safer. If it won't be leapt on when you feel you want to say sorry then you're much more likely to be able to say it.

It is also helpful for couples to think about different ways that sorry can be used. If it's felt that it's only about whether something was right or wrong, it can feel harder to say. 'Sorry, I got that wrong', can of course be a really helpful type of sorry. But there is also a type that couples find opens up a new dimension, which is 'I'm sorry that when I did X that it had that particular impact on you. I didn't realise it would.' This is less about who is right or wrong (always a tricky territory) and more about acknowledging the impact that something has had on one of them.

It isn't always easy to see what you need to say sorry for. But if the repairing conversation goes well and you give your partner a chance to explain themselves, you will probably hear what they think is your part in it. You may not find this comfortable to hear, or you may not agree with it, but letting your partner know that you are thinking about what they say will help them feel heard, and may make space for you in turn to explain what upset you.

It's going to depend on what works for you. If you were mending something you would choose a suitable thread or colour; in the same way, you can learn between you how best to repair with each other after you've disconnected in some way. This is something you can have a dynamic conversation about (though not in the middle of an argument), because you might feel differently from your partner about it. One of you might feel really soothed after an argument by physical touch, or a hug; one of you might need to go over the argument with words or might need a joke to lighten the mood.

It can also be helpful to think about language that attempts to repair things as they happen. If we have something difficult to tell our partner, we might think about how to phrase it in order to acknowledge the hurt it is going to cause. Sometimes, we think that if we don't acknowledge a difficulty, we can avoid it being difficult, but this may be optimistic ... finding a way to describe disappointed feelings and share them together rather than avoid them can help.

For example, when it comes to Josh, whom we met earlier, having to go off to work, he could say this in different ways.

Contrast:

JOSH: I'm going off to work now – say goodnight to the kids for me.
RYAN: Okay.

With

JOSH: I'm going off to work now. Sorry, I know this is hard on us – say goodnight to the kids for me.
RYAN: Yeah it is but thanks for saying that.

In the second example, Josh makes it explicit that it is hard on them both, which might make it easier for them to feel connected to each other at this point. Somehow, even in these micro conversations of daily life, the small gesture of acknowledging the impact that you might have on each other when you do something you know is going to be frustrating or disappointing can help create something more friendly and connected.

Ideas for reflection
- *Do you manage to reflect on an argument after it has happened?*
- *What helps you move on after an argument?*
- *What helps your partner move on after an argument?*
- *How safe do you feel about saying sorry in your relationship?*

Keeping safe

I've been talking here about disagreements and arguments between couples and how you go about repairing with each other. But clearly there is also the question of safe conflict and safe disagreement. I hope that some of the ideas in this chapter can help disagreements and difficult things be talked about constructively, but if issues and conflicts escalate to a point where one or both people in a relationship feel scared or out of control, or where your children are exposed to unresolved hostile conflict between you, it is essential to get proper help – I've listed some resources in Appendix 2. This may be where you are seeking help either individually or as a couple; the starting point is likely to be what feels safe for you.

Keeping safe may involve having agreements about how not to escalate things and about how you might together agree on strategies to cool things down when it feels as if they are getting heated. This to some degree will depend on what you are both like, individually.

Ideas that some couples have:

- If there are children, being able to think about the timing of conversations and being able to stop the argument before it gets heated.
- It being okay for one person to say 'we need to pause or stop the conversation as it's starting to get heated'.
- Steering the conversation away from blaming statements.
- Thinking about the role substances play in their arguments. If, for example, alcohol is a problem factor in escalating arguments regularly, then this may need to be seriously looked at.
- An agreement that if they are both feeling upset that they will allow some physical space between them.

Couples who struggle with keeping things safe along these lines may need professional help to avoid arguments becoming dangerous or harmful to them and their children.

Don't forget the good stuff

Talking about the good stuff is also crucial. You may feel less inhibited in telling your partner what irritates you about them or criticising them than in telling them what you like about them, particularly if in your family of origin this is the way things have generally been done. But telling one another the things you appreciate helps a couple to clarify what works for them both.

What about the washing-up?

When Ashley doesn't wash his plate in the way Evie has asked him to a thousand times, what might get to her is not so much the plate lying around dirty as the feeling that she's not being listened to or heard by him on something that matters to her. Feeling listened to is important to all of us, but for her it might feel particularly important if in the past she has experienced being ignored. Being listened to might feel like being respected or cared for.

Equally, when Evie goes on at him about the plate, Ashley might think she's a nag who just wants things her way, who doesn't care about him and who overreacts. We might wonder what his experience is of people telling him what to do.

There are different questions that a communication lens might help us to recognise:

- Is Evie hoping that Ashley will mind read her feelings about the washing-up? Or does she need to frame her request more actively?
- And if so, is there a way Evie could frame her request better – putting it in terms of what she feels rather than how hopeless she thinks Ashley is?

For example, 'When you leave your plate in the sink it really gets to me and I feel like you are leaving it because you know I'll just do it.' At least if she states what she is feeling then Ashley has a chance to take this on board and respond to her concerns. 'I really am not leaving it for you to do. I just don't think to say that. Perhaps if I did it would help?' In having this exchange, there is a chance for them to clarify things.

- Is Evie expressing her frustration about something else? Is this exchange about the washing-up a sign that something else needs tending to by having a difficult conversation that one or both of them has been avoiding?
- How can they make this conversation more bespoke to them? Is there a particular problem with tone? How does Ashley experience her tone? What about timing? Is there a better time to talk about this?

If Evie says 'I'll do it', but her tone is frustrated and she's just doing it to be a martyr, is this a sign that Ashley is supposed to pick up on? If Ashley ignores it, is that going to help them? How do they manage when one of them is sulking? Are they able to think about how to deal with it better?

As I said in the introduction, you cannot possibly think about all these aspects at the moment you are having an argument about the washing-up, but there may be different things going on that you could think about and maybe have a conversation about afterwards.

Summing up

We argue with our partners about the stuff we care about; the stuff that makes us or them upset or that feels important to either of us. We may have tried to communicate it in other ways and failed; or we may have tried to avoid communicating about it (and it has now found another way to reveal itself). If we can find better ways to listen to each other, and be more understanding of different ideas or styles of communicating, this may help us to pick up on the things that matter to each of us. If an issue keeps coming up, it clearly matters, and for the sake of the relationship a way needs to be found to engage with it.

While writing this book I had regular meetings on Zoom with a good friend and colleague to talk through my ideas. For some reason, there was a period when we kept ending up on different Zoom links. Each week we struggled. Sometimes I'd have to phone her to find out where she was. Eventually we'd get there, but at times we each felt a bit frustrated with the other. How hard could it be to just get on to the right link? We laughed when we realised how apt our struggles were for the theme of this chapter. Getting on to the same 'page' had involved more frustration and more work communicating about it than we had bargained for.

Similarly – and more intensely! – in our couple relationships, while we may think it should be easy to get on to the same 'page' as our partner, sadly, it takes work. This can be disappointing and frustrating if our deepest hope is that the person we love understands us without work. And if we assume that we know what our partner means all the time then we will also be disappointed. Assuming that we can finish each other's sentences is asking for problems.

It seems, therefore, that in order to move forward into a better way of communicating, we have to give up our ideas that our partners will get it right first time. Instead we need to enter into a not so smooth process involving patience and clarification, and possibly a few arguments, while we try to understand each other (and ourselves) better. How we talk to each other, how we listen to each other, and how we make a space to try to decode each other's behaviour (which is of course a form of communication) are all elements with which it can be really helpful to engage. In this way, we hope that trust can be built up in a forum in which we try to understand and be understood by each other. Finding a way into this forum is, in a sense, the 'argument that couples need to have' (with perhaps a lot of arguments on the way). This forum is also the place where difficult but necessary conversations can take place about what needs to be discussed. Within a relationship there will be different phases to this. The first is to ensure that the channel actually exists within the relationship (particularly given a natural tendency to avoid talking about difficult stuff); but then there's the job of maintaining the channel, keeping it flowing smoothly, and giving it time and attention.

What seems to work well for couples in this area
- *Making time to check in with each other regularly about how they are doing. Also linked to ...*

- *Actively making time to talk with each other about important or potentially difficult things at a time where they know they are going to be without distractions.*
- *Listening to each other's point of view without interrupting.*
- *Being aware of the things each finds difficult about communicating.*
- *Taking into account the communication styles they both learned in childhood.*
- *Finding helpful ways to say sorry.*
- *Not getting conversations off to a bad start with blame.*
- *Remembering to comment on the good things.*
- *Acknowledging what each other thinks or feels even if they don't agree with it. This is such an important one. It changes conversations that are rigid and defensive into conversations where they can each feel more understood.*

2

Family (aka 'your mother drives me crazy')

There are plenty of mother-in-law jokes, but for some couples the issue of the 'in-laws' is no joke at all, causing painful arguments and touching raw nerves.

Beena and Marco were a couple like this. They had a two-year-old son, Theo, and Beena was six months' pregnant. Marco's mother Sofia, who lived abroad, had come to stay with them in their flat in London for a month. The idea had been that she would come and help Beena who was feeling really tired, and spend some precious time with Theo. But, rather than Sofia's presence alleviating some of the pressure the couple felt, every night after Sofia had gone to bed, Beena and Marco would argue. Beena was furious about the way she felt Sofia was treating her. She found it rude that Sofia kept telling her to eat more healthily, saying that it wouldn't be good for the baby if she was eating crisps or chocolate all the time. Sofia had pointed out that when Marco had been a little boy, he had never been allowed snacks the way Theo was, and that he had been such a good boy who ate all his meals – unlike Theo who seemed so fussy. But what Beena was even more furious about, even more than what were to her intrusive comments, was that Marco wasn't sticking up for her. His mother shouldn't be allowed to tell her to do everything differently! This was her home! Marco, on the other hand, felt at a loss. What to do? He felt stuck between his wife and his mother since whatever he said he would offend one of them.

I want to look in this chapter at this 'in-law problem' in detail, as it seems to stand for a wider issue that all couples have to find a way to resolve – aka an 'argument they (need to) have'. Namely, how to cope with all the aspects of each other's family of origin* that enter into their relationship. This story between Beena and Marco (and I've heard a lot of Beena and Marco type scenarios) seems to capture the inevitable tensions we encounter when we come up against the culture of our partner's family and the way that they do things. Marco's mother's way of doing things is different from Beena's. This isn't the only thing that is problematic; it's also that these differences are felt to be intrusive and Beena doesn't feel able to manage this. Marco and Beena need to resolve the extent to which they can bear to allow his family's ways into their family. These are questions that won't go away; a person's family is part of them.

Meet the parents

The moment we 'meet the parents' is often deemed significant, but it represents only the beginning of a long and complex task of finding a way to deal with the reality

---

*By family of origin I mean the significant caregivers someone grew up with.

of each other's families and their ways. No longer are such 'ways' behind their own front doors. They are now coming to a town near you, namely, into your relationship.

The disagreements that couples bring to therapy in this area can be extremely painful and distressing. There's a 'close to the bone' feeling – and rightly so, because family is in our bones, deep down in us. At the same time they are 'arguments couples need to have' in order to find a way of being that works for 'this family', i.e. them, as a couple, that is about both of them as well as their wider families.

So in this chapter I'll look at some of these 'family-related' conflicts, which may not always be as obvious as they seem and don't always look like 'rows about the mother-in-law'. I'll think about what might be going on and also show that conflicts in this area may be normal and necessary: part of making a shift into being a couple and understanding each other better. I'll then come back to Beena and Marco.

What planet are you on?

A couple are arguing about whether to put in the plug and fill up the sink with water to do the washing-up, or to leave the tap running while they wash everything separately. They enjoy the banter around this difference between them. At the same time they sometimes feel that they are so very different, and there are times when it feels frustrating.

Without adding the context of the way these individuals have grown up, we may miss something about this source of tension and fail to really understand these firmly held views. It turns out that it is ingrained in the 'sink filler upper' to conserve water. She grew up in a country where easy access to fresh water was not taken for granted and every day it was drummed into her by her mother how important it was to save water. This is very different from the experience of her partner, who grew up never thinking about this issue.

When we come up against a partner's firmly held view that clashes with our own, we may be confronting something very old in them. This may relate to the way things have been done in their family that differs to the way they've been done in our own. At some level, we may have been drawn to them for these very differences. But equally, it can feel really hard to get our heads around them. As one client said – it can often feel as if we're from different planets.

Some couples really worry about this. There is an idea that they should feel the same about things in order to be properly compatible. But even if we grew up on the same street in houses next door to each other in the same wider culture, our family atmosphere is likely to be different.

It makes me think of hanging out with friends when my children and theirs were babies. Even though in lots of ways we were similar and had things in common, the way we all parented was individual and unique. The way we fed our babies, held them, spoke to them, played with them. What we did for fun with the babies, what we did for down time. The way we comforted them when they were sad or couldn't sleep. The rules we had and the approach to time management. The amount of mess we could tolerate. The way we and our partners worked together and how we dealt with disagreements. There was no question – we all loved our babies and were doing our best, but we all had our different ways and all brought our different hopes for what we could offer our children.

Fast forward and I imagine these babies as adults, trying to get together in relationships with one another and working out their contrasting ways of doing things – ways that can seem so different in areas that may feel integral to their sense of themselves. Every family in the world has its own feel, its own atmosphere, its own rules, its own unique climate. As a child growing up in any particular family you will inevitably inhale from that individual atmosphere ideas about how things get done – everything from how to eat to how to show love (or not) or how long it is acceptable to spend in the toilet. You don't necessarily have to agree with those ideas, and as you grow up you will develop your own point of view – keeping some things and reacting against others. You may also have a particular experience of how the world treats your family and how easy or difficult it has been for them in the world. All these ideas and experiences will exist somewhere inside the grown-up child who is now an adult. And when that grown-up child gets together with someone else, they have to find a way to manage and learn about each other's different perspectives. In this soup of deep-down differences in the ways we do and think about things, as well as a potential richness there is also huge potential for culture shock and disagreements. These differences may relate to the wider cultures we've grown up in and in cultures specific to our family (which will be also affected by the wider culture in which the family lives). Getting to know these differences and these aspects of each other is a long and inevitably bumpy journey.

Why are you doing it like that (or why aren't you doing it like that)?

Mel wrings out the cloth automatically after they do the washing-up, and it irritates her every time that her partner Rosa doesn't think to do this. Rosa, on the other hand, feels irritated that Mel doesn't stack the cutlery head up in the dishwasher.

Kaleb thinks the weekends are for doing nothing. He doesn't mind the children crashing out in front of the TV for as long as they want to. Laura thinks this is a terrible idea, and every weekend they argue about it.

Meg is a planner and likes to book tickets way in advance. Pete finds this annoyingly organised and would rather be spontaneous.

Nelly and Luis struggle with finding a holiday they both want to go on. Nelly doesn't want to go away with friends as she feels it's not at all restful and hates all the compromises required. Luis thinks holidays are for socialising.

Most couples have their version of these differences (or at least the couples I've worked with do, and I certainly have my own version of them in my relationship). These clashes of ideas about how to do things appear in my sessions with couples again and again, sometimes driving them mad, sometimes leaving them worrying that they're incompatible, and often making them think that their partner is thoughtless, uncaring or controlling because they don't seem willing or able to do these things any other way. Why is it so hard for you to understand how important this is to me?!

One way of thinking about these differences constructively might be to use a 'family' lens, to see how these differences of ideas might be rooted in the way we've been brought up, whether from the way things have been done in our families or because we've reacted against how they were done. Meg may be a planner not because her family were all planners but because everything was chaotic in her family, which left her feeling that she wanted (or needed) to do things differently. If Nelly came from a family who didn't go on holiday, if she had had no siblings or was the child of a single parent, she may have had less experience than Luis of being in a big group and is perhaps more apprehensive.

Being curious with each other about our different approaches and experiences lets us start to plot these differences within the context of our families. Just because we've always had a certain way of doing things based on the way things have been done (or not done) in our backgrounds, it doesn't mean that is the right way (even if it really feels as if it is). It also doesn't necessarily mean that our partner is setting out to be difficult (even if it really feels as if they are) when they are different. Now that we are in a couple, we may have to expand our range to include a whole new set of ideas about the little things (let alone the big things, which I'll come to).

A typical weekend row between Kaleb and Laura might go:

LAURA: You don't really care, do you, about the kids
    rotting their brains on TV all weekend.
KALEB: They work really hard all week! Why can't you
    give us all a break!?
LAURA: They should be outside doing stuff or making
    things or reading.
KALEB: Well I think they should also be relaxing.

There is a real value for the kids in having parents who can think together about the different ideas they have. But this debate leaves both Laura and Kaleb exasperated. Is there a way in which thinking about it together in the context of their family backgrounds could unlock some of the tension here?

LAURA: The truth of it is that I felt like my parents
    plonked me in front of the TV at any opportunity.
    I spent hours watching rubbish on my own and
    I don't think it did me any good. I want it to be
    different for our kids.
KALEB: I see. I guess that is different from my
    experience. I have really good warm memories of
    watching TV as a family. We all used to sit together
    every night and it felt nice, it was comfortable and
    good watching something together.

This kind of conversation gives background to what might seem like a very concrete 'my way or your way' exchange. When you start to see these layers of each other (and of yourself) it can help to take the tension out of the conversation. Through the comparison of differences (rather than a competition for one of you to win or the chance to 'be right') you might learn something about yourself and have a new perspective on something that has always been an absolute given to you.

While we are comfortable with what is familiar to us (I think of the *'family'* in *familiar*), we may also be yearning for something different. In the tension of our differences we may learn from each other, if we can bear not to be outraged or offended by the differences. Meg and Pete, for example, may be able to rub off on each other, when it comes to the tensions between early planning and spontaneity. Kaleb and Laura's kids may get the benefit of both of their parents' ideas here. There is a potential in this crucible that holds all that we both bring from our families.

Ideas for reflection
- *Are there habits or ways of doing everyday things that you and your partner often clash over?*
- *Can you relate any of your ideas about how things should be done to how things were done in your own families?*

Food
Food is such a vivid and rich area in which family differences come up. So many aspects of food can feel at odds in a couple – what we like to eat, when we want to eat, the way we eat and cook, the way we hold our cutlery, the way we tidy up (or don't), the manners we've been brought up with around food, even how we store it. Some of these may relate to aspects of ourselves that relate to our

earliest experiences of relationships in our family – some of which may predate our memories. The way we were fed, how easy we found it, how our caregivers felt about it and dealt with it, the food our parents made for us – all of this goes into making us who we are. We all have our own hugely personal relationship with food and it is something that is woven into every single day of our lives. When we get into a relationship with someone, and even more so when we live together, food is likely to become an area that is shared yet is so personal: shopping, cooking, eating, clearing up (as if any of you who spent lockdown with your partner need me to remind you). When you encounter your partner's feelings and attitudes about food and eating (which includes the joy, or not, of seeing and hearing them eat, but more of that in chapter 5), you are encountering something very personal to them. Sometimes there can be a wonderful richness to the sharing of ideas about food, a sensory pleasure and a repeated shared experience that can bring couples together. But sometimes it can become a place of difficulty because of the depths of ideas that people have about food and eating.

Lee and Conan were a couple who sought help with arguments they were having. They felt they were different in many ways and were worried about incompatibility. One of the arguments they had was about their different approaches to sitting down and eating together. Lee felt that Conan wasn't interested in mealtimes. While Lee wanted to sit down and eat together at the end of the day, Conan said he felt tired and that that was the last thing he felt like doing.

From the sound of it Lee was a very competent cook

who put a lot of energy and dedication into preparing and cooking food. He said this was how things were done in his family. Indeed, when I had initially asked him to describe a picture from his childhood for me, this was what he had immediately described – the picture of his family at the end of the day round the kitchen table. He said his dad would come home and his mum would have made the dinner and they would go straight to eating. This was how everyone reconnected at the end of a busy day. This, he said, was something he really wanted to recreate in his own relationship.

Conan had a different relationship with food. He said it wasn't a big deal in his family. He was one of five children and he remembered comings and goings and people helping themselves to whatever was available. His parents both worked shifts so there wasn't a set time for everyone to sit down. He sometimes found it frustrating that Lee was so adamant about them sitting down to eat or eating something elaborate. For him, home life really wasn't about food. He also hated all the clearing up that went with Lee doing elaborate cooking.

Having the conversation about it in the context of their family attitudes to food was illuminating. Not only did it help them understand each other better, but it also drew attention to some sadness on Lee's part. He spoke about how much he was missing his family, who lived abroad. He missed home, he said, not only the food culture of home but the whole way of life with his family and friends. Conan said that he wanted Lee to feel that home was here, with him. Lee said he was really struggling with that. This conversation about different attitudes to eating had led them into something more poignant and painful that needed addressing between them. Sometimes it is in the everyday things that we learn something important, and we can only get to these important feelings by taking time to understand what is going on when our partner feels different to us.

This struggle about mealtimes wasn't the only issue between them, but opening up the conversation about it certainly brought depth and understanding to an important area that they hadn't been able to go into with each other before. It also gave them a chance to think about what could be negotiated between them to find a way through. Conan understood better how much it meant to Lee for him to sit down and eat and was willing to try harder on this, but only if Lee could better appreciate how frustrating Conan found all the mess. Seeing their different ideas through the lens of their family contexts seemed to take the heat out of the tensions.

Ideas for reflection
- *What place did food and eating have in your families? What were your experiences of eating? Are there family stories about you in relation to food?*
- *What are the feelings about food and eating in your current relationship?*
- *Does this link back to any ideas about food and eating within your family of origin?*

Why don't you ever show me you care?
Our families provide our earliest experiences of being cared for (or not), so we may bring different ideas of how

we want to be cared for and how we want care to be shown to our relationships.

Lisa and Eliot had come for help as Lisa was feeling quite alone and unsupported in the relationship. A theme that came up in our sessions was about how they showed each other that they cared. She felt that Eliot never showed her he cared. This was something Lisa often got upset about, nursing a sense of unfairness and resentment, as she felt she showed him a lot of care. I asked him if he felt that he did show Lisa he cared. He said that it was funny, he felt as if he was always trying to do so but that it didn't seem enough. He described how he would come into the house and tidy up all the shoes and bags that the kids had left on the floor, putting them away neatly as he knew it drove Lisa mad that it was messy. He did this for her; he didn't even want acknowledgement, but it made him feel sad to hear her telling him he didn't care.

When I asked them how love and care had been shown in each of their families, Lisa said that it had always been presents. Whatever their financial situation, which hadn't always been good, somehow her dad was always coming home with a gift or a balloon or a present from somewhere he had been to show he'd been thinking about her. She was sad as she spoke about it, saying that she missed him very much after his death.

Eliot said that it hadn't been like that in his family. 'You showed love by working hard and not causing any trouble,' he said. His parents, like Lisa's, had had traditional roles and his dad had worked long hours to support them all; this was how Eliot said his dad had showed love. Presents weren't really a feature for them. Eliot said he guessed this was his role model here – 'you did your bit, you worked hard, you tried to keep the show on the road', whether that was clearing up the messy shoes or going out to work. He had thought he was doing the best he could.

A conversation like this can help a couple shift something and help them realise that while it may feel that their partner is always getting it wrong (or they are), there may be understandable reasons for why they keep trying to put their 'square peg' version of love and care into the 'round hole' space. This question of how you show care in a relationship is so important. One of our deepest longings is to be cared for, and we hope that our partners will offer us the kind of care we are looking for, without us always being able to say what that is.

We have to be prepared for the fact that our partner may not understand our idea of care even when it is spelled out to them – that it may be completely different from their idea of how you show someone you love them. A feeling that 'whatever I try never seems enough' might be a clue that there are different expectations about what love or care might look like. There may be deeper feelings here too, which I will come to in a bit, but for now it might be helpful to map out ways in which each of you might like the other to show love or care. It might be gestures such as presents, something more physical or tactile, showing that you care by making an effort with your appearance, saying it in words, working hard, keeping the house tidy, or something that will probably relate to the way in which you've had love or care shown (or not shown) when growing up.

Ideas for reflection
- *How did love and care get shown in your family when you were growing up?*
- *Does this differ between you and your partner?*
- *How do you like to be shown love and care?*

What is your idea of a couple?

We may have our different ideas from family about everyday things – how best to do the washing-up or what mealtimes should be like. But we may also have different ideas about things that are less concrete. What should a couple be like? What is a good relationship? What does having children mean for a relationship? How important is sex to a relationship? When is a relationship not working? The ideas we have about relationships from our family are so important. When I meet a couple for the first time, one of the areas I like to think about is what examples of relationships they have in their minds. What was their parents' relationship like, and their grandparents' relationship? What are the role models they do or don't have? Their ideas about relationships may be completely different.

Anya and Ben came for therapy to discuss some of their differences about settling down and starting a family. Ben was really keen to start a family but Anya said that though she felt committed to Ben, and knew that she would like children at some point, she was in no hurry. She said that she was thirty-one and had plenty of time. For now, her career was more important. Ben felt that she was sticking her head in the sand. He was concerned about her age – what if they struggled to conceive? He also felt it undermined his sense of security in the relationship. Perhaps she wasn't as serious as he was about it.

Thinking about the 'couples' they had in their minds as examples of how a relationship should be gave them a way into thinking about their different concerns. Anya said that there had always been a frostiness between her parents. She'd never quite understood it but she had the feeling that her mum had resented giving up her job to look after Anya and her brother. She saw that her mum felt she never had her own money, even though her dad was always saying that their money was shared. Anya was adamant that she would have her own career; she wasn't going to be stuck in the position her mum was in. This was all relevant to her concerns now as she was worried about what having a baby would mean for her career. She felt that she needed to be more established in her job to be able to think about taking some time out.

As for Ben's parents' relationship, he said that it was not something he would like to copy. He felt that they hadn't had a particularly happy relationship, but in his view had 'stayed together' for him and his two brothers. They had then split up as soon as his youngest brother had left school, which 'had been a relief to all of them'. Anya's holding off on wanting a baby was worrying him. Perhaps it was a sign she had doubts about the relationship. In the context of their previous experiences of family, it was understandable that both of them had worries about becoming a family. Airing their worries alongside each other was really important so that their ideas could be 'reality tested' within the setting of their own relationship.

For example, Anya's deep certainty that 'she wasn't

going to be stuck in the position her mum was in' was important for them to address together rather than for Anya to hold on to on her own. Her opening up about this meant that Ben was able to address the concern with her. Equally Ben being honest about his insecurity about the relationship meant that Anya was more able to reassure him on that front. It was going to be important for him to work out which of his feelings here related to the relationships he'd seen growing up and which belonged to his current relationship.

This work took some time between us, as they spoke and thought about these issues together. While they had initially seemed to be polarised in their ideas – with Ben being the one who was keen to have a baby and Anya the one holding them back – they moved into a safer zone where both could be open about their mixed feelings. It turned out that there was a part of Anya that she didn't really know about herself that was yearning to have a baby but she had been frightened to allow that part of her any airtime. It had seemed safer for Ben to express the wish. Similarly, Ben also had his own fears about becoming a parent. Their conversation expanded. By being able to talk about their mixed feelings it made them feel more supportive of each other.

After working with me for about a year, they said that they had a deeper understanding of each other and felt somehow freer to shape their own relationship rather than be preoccupied with having a relationship like their parents. This didn't mean that they had all the answers yet or had made a decision, but it seemed clearer to them so they could work out what belonged where.

These ideas we may have about couple relationships can act as a template or a road map that we may or may not wish to follow. If we can tune in to these ideas in ourselves and in each other, we can become more aware of how they shape our thoughts and expectations, and have a more active conversation about whether we want to replicate or avoid aspects of our parents' relationships – whether we want to go along their road map.

The models we have inherited from family will resonate with us in our relationships in different ways. Sometimes these will be very subtle whispers that need a careful ear; sometimes they will be noisier and more obvious. The ideas for reflection that follow are questions that I often think about with couples in this area. I am aware that everyone has their own family experience and some may not have had two parents or may not have been brought up by their parents; whatever the experience, it is all important to be able to tune into it within the relationship.

Ideas for reflection
- *How would you describe the relationships in your family?*
- *Do you have fears or hopes based on the model of their relationships?*
- *Do you have other models of a couple that appeal to you or that you wouldn't want to follow?*
- *How did your family communicate with one another and how does that affect your ideas about how to communicate?*
- *How did your parents deal with problems between them?*

- *How did your parents handle their separation and what do you understand of the reasons for their separation (if applicable to your family)?*

Why do you always have to overreact?

It's not just the models of relationships that you've grown up with that might need mapping. Everyone having a unique and individual family experience means that everyone has their unique sore points or sensitivities: places where they may have been hurt or felt let down. Often it is only in the intense closeness of a couple relationship that these sensitivities show themselves. These experiences may create substantive worries or fears about what being in a relationship is going to mean for us, about whether it is even possible. But they may also create worries or fears about the small things. For example, if you have grown up feeling that your family aren't that interested in you, then you might feel particularly sensitive to your partner seeming dismissive when they are looking at their phone. Ashley feels Evie overreacts to the washing-up being left around, but perhaps she has history that makes her sensitive to a feeling of not being thought about, and could relate this experience to the plate being left in the sink. Or if perhaps someone has grown up in a violent or aggressive atmosphere, it may feel very threatening or dangerous to hear an expression of anger from their partner.

People will often say to me about their partner – 'it's so weird, I never feel this upset/angry/hurt with anyone else' but it's only in the very close atmosphere of a love relationship that these old sore points can be touched and can really hurt, often to the bafflement of the other person.

It's hard living with someone's unique sore points without any guide to them. It's like driving across rough ground for the first time without any idea where the holes or bumps are, and only realising that you've driven into a hole when your partner is screaming in pain. Being in a relationship is a slow process of coming to know this terrain, and working out if you can manage it.

So when we say 'your family drives me crazy' it also stands for the 'family' that lives inside a person. Because this family experience inside someone is so old and so much a part of them it can really be something that their partner feels they meet time and time again.

Nathan and Ella had come for therapy to improve their relationship, which they felt was sometimes good but sometimes very argumentative and spiky. Nathan often brought up Ella's lateness and her lack of organisation as something he struggled with. He felt she needed to 'grow up' and take more responsibility; he wasn't prepared to be constantly dealing with her chaos and not getting any thanks from her for this. Nathan was really struggling – he couldn't see how she failed to see the impact on him of her behaviour.

I asked Ella if she herself felt this was something she struggled with. She said that her family had always picked her up on it, that she'd felt labelled by them as slightly chaotic and hopeless, unlike her brother who seemed to be more organised. Indeed she had a general sense that her brother was more competent than her – he had been something of a golden boy. When she and Nathan argued about it, she said he could make her feel really bad. She knew this was a really difficult area for her but she tried and hoped that it wouldn't get in the way of their relationship. She worried that if she always apologised to him about it then it might turn it into more of an issue.

This seemed to be a really important problem between them that needed to be better understood. Zoning in on Ella's relationship with her brother gave both of them a deeper level of awareness about her. She said that it was such an old feeling to feel hopeless compared with her brother. Nathan's complaint really hit a nerve. When he complained, she felt an old sense of rivalry with her brother rise up, which played out between her and Nathan. She also felt bad, and wanted to defend herself against feeling so bad. With these layers to the story Nathan could cater better for the impact he had on her when he brought up this complaint. He said perhaps he needed to go more gently. When he did, she didn't feel the need to defend herself so much. This took the heat out of the conversation and also created a space for Nathan to speak about the impact she had on him when she was late. He said that he sometimes really panicked. She hadn't known this about him. In fact, she was inadvertently touching one of his sore spots whenever she was late. It was helpful for them to see that when they were more aware of each other's vulnerabilities, the spikiness between them subsided.

It was also interesting that they had chosen one another. The differences between them, while feeling like incompatibility, actually gave them a chance to work something through and develop. Ella, because she felt

Nathan was sympathetic to her (notwithstanding that he was frustrated), began to think more about the impact she had on him when she was late. Nathan too was able to share a part of him that he normally kept hidden and could feel that it was okay to do that.

Starting to get a grip on each other's emotional landscape, starting to map out each other's sore points, can help a couple stop hurting each other in the same place again and again, which is what can happen unless they look at why they always react in the same way to things. This mapping out business, like zoning in on the map app on your phone to see a place so close up that you can even see the buildings, is something that can happen in a dynamic way. Sometimes it's someone becoming more aware of themself, and finding a way to convey that to their partner. Sometimes it's their partner helping them become more aware of themself, and then both of them increasing in awareness. As the terrain becomes better known, it's often a relief when a couple start to understand the impact that they can have on each other, which then gives them more scope to try to change it or at least to acknowledge the pain it can cause.

This is so not what I hoped it would be

The frustrations and disappointments of our early relationships, whether with our parents, siblings, or other people close to us, can leave their mark and affect our hopes and wishes for our later relationships. The urge to repeat (or avoid) something familiar from our early relationships may lead us (without us even realising it) towards people who have something about them that appeals at a deeper level in terms of our previous experiences (and they may have been led to us for the same reasons).

This is why we might see someone (possibly even ourselves) ending up in a familiar dynamic in relationships with different people, or why perhaps we seem to have a 'type'. Just at the moment when we think we are getting away from our families, their legacy may be guiding the relationship choices that we make. This can act positively or negatively, but being aware of it is helpful. And if we can think about the hopes and expectations that we may have about our partners, and understand that some of them we won't even be aware of, we can see that it is a huge and probably impossible task for any relationship to fulfil them. Our longings may be powerful and overwhelming. They can make people feel that their partner isn't acceptable, without really knowing why they feel that. Sometimes it works the other way – the hope for a relationship is so strong that it overrides the fact that the relationship might not really be working. What I often address is the question of whether these mismatches of expectations can be tolerated within the relationship. Can someone live with the idea that their relationship hasn't repaired what they hoped it would? Can this be mourned between them so that they can find a way to live with the disappointment that it is not what they hoped it would be?

I might hear something like 'I'm faced with the huge disappointment that this is not what I thought it was going to be – but now I look at what I was hoping for and I realise it was connected to the sadnesses of my growing up. It's painful to think of those things that I long for.' But a more realistic relationship can take place when we let go of an idealised version, and find a way to incorporate disappointments with what is enjoyed and shared.

Vicki and Sean came for therapy after Sean discovered that Vicki had been having an affair with a colleague. They had been together for twenty years and had teenage children. Both were hugely distressed by the situation and sought help to support them through the crisis in which they found themselves. Vicki had ended the affair and said that she wanted to try to save their marriage. Sean was devastated and said that he didn't know what he wanted to do but coming to therapy seemed like a place to start.

When I'm working with a couple where an affair has been discovered, it is a complex job to tend to the intense feelings of pain, betrayal and guilt as well as trying to understand what has happened and why. In Vicki's case, it seemed that in her affair she had found a sense of freedom that she felt she didn't have in her relationship with Sean. She said that she had found Sean critical and demanding of her and felt she was never allowed to express herself in the way she wanted. The colleague with whom she had been having the affair 'didn't make any demands' of her and this was a feeling she said she yearned for.

When we thought about this in the context of Vicki's family background, she said that her mother had probably had undiagnosed depression for her whole life and that the atmosphere at home was always tense. Her father was quite strict and family life revolved round not causing any trouble or upset. It seemed she'd longed 'to have a space without any demands on her' for many years, long before her relationship with Sean. Sean felt she wasn't being fair to him; that he wasn't as demanding as she thought he was.

It was a long and complex process to figure out what feelings belonged where. There were lots of questions to contemplate. Had Vicki chosen to marry someone a bit like her dad in order to have a chance to repair something familiar? Or was she placing her ideas about her relationship with her dad on to Sean? Was Sean unaware of how he came across? Had they avoided conversations about their feelings? Had the affair been a way of dealing with that? On Sean's side there were questions too. What did betrayal mean to him? Had he been drawn to Vicki for reasons that related to his experiences? Betrayal seemed to have been a theme in his family; his father had an affair when he was nine and it had ended his parents' marriage.

Sean said it was a shame that they were talking about these important questions only after a crisis had forced them to. Vicki said that being aware of their different feelings made her feel closer to Sean than she had for a long time. Sean, on the other hand, felt that he needed space to process what had happened; that it was all so painful and was bringing up older unhappy feelings for him, and for now he wanted to figure out what he wanted to do on his own.

The affair had clearly brought a lot to the surface about their own families. In order for them to move forward, whether together or apart, the questions that the affair had posed in relation to their older family experiences needed some attention. In a way, they needed to look backwards to be able to make that movement forward.

Becoming aware of the landscape of your longings and

disappointments can help to sift out which belong to old relationships and which belong to what's happening now. Of course, this is a task in itself, and is one of the things that individual therapy can offer, by giving someone space to think (and indeed, Sean sought his own therapy).

It may be a crisis event like an affair but it may be something less momentous. When you or your partner experience a moment where one of you seems disproportionately upset or angry about something that has just happened and the one on the receiving end can't get their head around why it's had such a huge impact, this dynamic is a clue that perhaps this is about an older feeling. Couples come and tell me that they have 'baggage', a phrase used to encompass all of these old feelings or disappointments. If we are going to use that phrase then I like to think of 'baggage handling' as being something important that couples need to do with each other – they can't get away from each other's baggage, but they can handle it more carefully by having a greater understanding of what it comprises.

Ideas for reflection
- *What attracted you to each other?*
- *What do you feel you are looking for in a relationship?*
- *If you feel disappointed, can you think about why you feel disappointed, and where your expectations might come from?*

Your mother drives me crazy
Back to Beena and Marco. Given the thinking in the rest of this chapter, we might now be in a better place to put their

argument in the context of seeing that couples inevitably struggle with aspects of one another's family (whatever those aspects look like). The challenge for them will be to find a way to deal *as a couple* with the problems caused by Marco's mother's arrival, rather than feeling that it is the other person who needs to solve the problem.

In this first example, it is as if they feel it is the other person's responsibility to find a solution.

BEENA: I can't do this any more – there's nothing I can do that's right. She only wants to criticise me.

MARCO: Don't let her get to you. She means well! She just wants to cook us some food and she cares that the baby is healthy. [Marco implying that it's Beena who needs to change here – by not letting it get to her.]

BEENA: You have to say something to her. I need you to stick up for me. It's making me so tense. [Beena thinking that it's Marco who has to sort it by sticking up for her.]

MARCO: How can I say something? She's come all this way and we should make her feel welcome. It's not right to do that. It's only going to create upset which is going to be counter-productive.

BEENA: Typical – you are always going to take her side, aren't you.

MARCO: Well, she is my mother. I think you've got to get your head round that.

BEENA: But where do I fit in here?

MARCO: Look, she is only here for two more weeks, and then it will go back to normal.

BEENA: But this is my home too! And I'm pregnant! And there's nowhere I can get away from her in our flat! You should be thinking about me and my mental health!

MARCO: What about when your parents are here? At least my mother bothers to actually try and help us.

Ouch. This conversation between them is painful and is getting personal.

The problem they have is symbolic of the problems discussed elsewhere in the chapter. Sofia's way of doing things, and Marco's way of speaking to his mother, are indicative at some level of the 'way' in which things are done in his family – whether that's food or communicating. These clash with Beena's ideas – but this is now a problem not just for Beena, or not just for Marco. This is a problem for both of them.

If Beena and Marco stay in a position where they both consider that their position is immovable, it's going to be tricky for them to get beyond this argument. This makes it difficult, given that when it comes to issues around one's family it can be hard not to feel that there is a 'right' way of doing things. If Marco has never stood up to his mother, or if it isn't in his culture to do so, whether that's the internal culture of his family or the broader external culture, then it is going to feel very 'wrong' from his point of view to do so. Or if not wrong, then at least hard, or strange, or frightening. But Beena feels that he isn't respecting their relationship (or her) if he perpetuates the culture of his family. In this there is an intense clash of family cultures.

How can they shift away from being so polarised

about this? A more helpful approach might be to try to acknowledge the inevitable complexity of their situation and be more interested in the fears and worries that the other one has. This goes back to some of the thinking in the previous chapter about communication, with an emphasis on acknowledgement and trying to listen to where the other one is coming from.

BEENA: I can't help but feel criticised when she says I shouldn't be eating crisps. She makes me feel like I'm a terrible mother already. [Beena now talking in terms of how it makes her feel.]

MARCO: I'm sorry – I know I tell you to just brush it off but clearly it really gets to you. [Marco acknowledging.]

BEENA: It does, it really upsets me, and perhaps touches a nerve – maybe I am a bad mother, maybe I am afraid of that? And I feel like you are only interested in avoiding conflict with her, rather than supporting me.

MARCO: I just don't want to make a big deal out of it with her. That isn't really our way in our family – we don't argue. Everyone keeps quiet. I hate that but it's how it's always been. That's what I like about you and me – that we can be honest with each other. I hate this feeling of being in between you both. I feel worn out trying to keep you both happy. It's exhausting. [Marco able to speak about how he is feeling here.]

BEENA: It helps me to hear that. I do understand it's not easy for you. I don't think you need to keep us both happy – it's impossible. I do realise that. But it's different now. You aren't just a son any more. You are my partner and you are a dad. Equally, I guess I need to realise that you aren't just my husband.

MARCO: I think that I can speak to her about it, but I need to go sensitively, and I need your support with that.

BEENA: Sure. I can't promise that I won't feel upset, but it will mean a huge amount to me to know that you are trying.

The conversation between them has grown in dimension. Instead of there being the two starkly opposing ideas (either 'keep your mother out' or 'my relationship with my family is going to stay completely the same even though I now have a family of my own', both of which seem potentially unrealistic positions to hold on to) there are more nuances to their thinking about the situation, and this creates a more compassionate conversation. For example, when Marco admits to his own dissatisfaction with not feeling able to speak openly with his family, Beena can be more sympathetic.

The conversation growing in dimension doesn't take the issue away, but it means that they can be more understanding of each other and therefore more able to find a way through the issue together as a couple. In this instance they've decided that this means Marco is going to have a word with his mum. But I'm not saying that 'confronting the in-laws' is necessarily the 'right' outcome. This is going to depend on the specific family and the culture of the family. Being able to cope with the issue might mean not trying to change the situation; instead it might mean finding a way for the couple to better understand each other's family culture and to find a way of acceptance by connecting with each other over how hard they find their situation. However, this is still a *joint* process.

What does have to happen (whatever that looks like) is that potentially they must give up their own particular idea of what the answer is. Which is hard to do. Giving things up is painful. But it's easier to do if someone knows how hard it is for you. So if Beena is going to give up the idea that her mother-in-law won't have anything to do with her family, she may find it easier if Marco acknowledges the fact that how his mother behaves will create some uncomfortable moments for her. And if Marco is going to give up an idea that he won't ever speak to his mother about the way she gets involved, and that she will always expect him to behave as a son (without reference to his new role within his new family) then it will help if Beena is sympathetic to how hard that is for him.

In creating this more collaborative way of thinking that acknowledges the different fears and worries, it becomes possible for new perspectives to emerge. If Beena feels less under threat from Marco and his family, she may be more able to enjoy the care and concern coming from his mother, to see it not as an attack on her but as an expression of a wish to help and support her through her pregnancy. They can also make some of their own longings more known about. Marco appears to have some sadness about not being able to talk openly with his mother. This may be something about which, in his relationship with

Beena, he can find some relief as he becomes able to speak more collaboratively or openly.

When you're around your family it's as if you become a different person

Although it's the mother-in-law issue that often gets stereotyped as something couples struggle with, there may be other family relationships that can cause tension. Perhaps a sibling relationship that has been very close may need recalibrating within the context of a new relationship. For example, someone who has always spoken to her sister every day or seen her every weekend may think that this will continue when she is in a couple relationship. It won't be something she will think about changing until her partner says 'this needs to change'. Things then need to be renegotiated between them. Now sister one has a different significant relationship in her life, sister two will need to find a way to deal with that. Sister one will need to deal with it too, and her partner will need to understand what this means to her.

I often hear the complaint 'when you're around your family you behave like a different person'. It can be hard for someone to see their partner in a role that they aren't aware of. There are tensions here – as with Marco, the son who is now a dad and a partner, or a sister who is now in a close relationship with someone else. There is recalibrating to be done for all involved. Beena has to see Marco in the context of his family, and Marco potentially has to recalibrate his relationship with his mother so that she comes to understand that he has different roles now. These shifts and recalibrations may be painful, but if the couple can bear with each other and work it out together (rather than thinking that it's the other one's problem) then their feelings can be better processed.

Caring responsibilities

Another area in which a couple may struggle with the reality of each other's families is if they take on caring responsibilities for a member of their family, often for parents. The practical and emotional realities of taking on an increased caring role can be huge for a couple, and the 'younger' couple (often with childcaring responsibilities of their own) can feel pressure from both sides. Acknowledging the impact this caring role may have on their relationship can help a couple to keep a sense of connectedness.

Rasna was really struggling with the reality of Hari's recently increased caring responsibilities for his parents. Moving into more suitable accommodation involved a lot of work that was taking up his time and headspace. Rasna felt that she had more on her plate than usual with the kids, but given that this was his family and she was entirely supportive of him being involved in their care, she hardly felt able to bring this up as an issue . However, one evening she snapped at him about how hard it was for her and how he wasn't thinking of her enough.

This conversation could easily turn defensive:

HARI: Are you really going to put more pressure on me at this point? What about you thinking of me? You barely acknowledge me at the moment.

RASNA: Well, that's because I'm so busy with all the other stuff.

But it could go another way and be an opportunity to connect and share some of the pain of the situation.

HARI: I'm sorry, this is so hard on us.
RASNA: I know, and I know there's nothing that can be done, I'm just feeling a bit alone at the moment.
HARI: I know, me too.
RASNA: I just feel like we need to work a bit harder to keep in touch with each other at the moment.

There's not much they can do to change the situation, but the intimacy of knowing they both feel lonely means they can try to put it right, even if that isn't going to be easy. This 'shared mourning' may help them feel they have more resources to get through this situation together.

My ex drives us crazy

Another area of family life that causes conflict and pain is to do with previous relationships, whether it's an ex-partner or children.

Amber and Greg had had an affair which ended their respective marriages, causing much pain and upset, however happy and excited they were about their new relationship. Amber had two young children who lived with her and Greg had two teenage children who stayed with him every other weekend. Because of their responsibilities to their children they had decided not to move in together yet but they spent time together on some of the weekends with all of the children.

Recently, one of Greg's children had shown one of Amber's children something on the internet that Amber felt was too adult and they'd had a big row about it. Amber had found out because her ex-husband had told her about it and been really cross with her. Amber was starting to feel overwhelmed by the complexities of their new network of relationships. As a result they sought help.

Clearly there was a lot for Amber and Greg to figure out. There were painful realities to deal with and a lot of strong feelings, not just their own, but also their children's and those of their exes. The strong feelings often ended up being directed at each other: Amber's fears about the impact of her divorce on her children and how to get on with Greg's children often ended up being directed at Greg in an angry way; and Greg's frustration at how difficult the situation seemed to be often ended up being directed at Amber – 'if only you didn't have to make this so difficult for me'.

The relationship was harder than they had imagined it was going to be. With so much to process, they decided to take a break from each other (and from therapy) to focus on their own feelings about it. They used the therapy to think about this together and we talked about how both perhaps needed to take time to mourn the end of their previous relationships before getting into the complexities of another, and that maybe this would be helpful for all involved, including their children. It wasn't clear what taking a break would mean for their relationship (and I didn't find out what then happened between them, as often happens in my work) but they both felt it would help and both asked for help to find their own individual therapists.

Their example demonstrates how hard it can be for a

couple to find a way to incorporate each other's previous relationships, particularly where there is an ongoing relationship with a co-parent. Just as with a family of origin, this has to be negotiated not as individuals but as partners.

Families and washing-up

When Ashley doesn't do the washing-up in the way Evie wants and they argue about it, what might we learn by looking at it through the lens of their family experiences? I might ask questions such as:

- What family attitudes and ways of doing things do they bring to this?
- What template of communication do they have from their parents about doing the chores and how do they feel about those templates?
- Does this issue hit a nerve based on their family experiences? For example, is Ashley feeling that his nagging mum has reappeared? Is Evie sensitive to not being listened to or thought about?

Let's imagine a scenario where Evie's family members have a view on how to do the washing-up. How might Evie and Ashley cope with this? Could they have a helpful conversation in order to manage the tension around the involvement of their families?

Summing up

When I start working with a couple I always ask if they can give me a feel of the families they grew up in, and what the atmosphere was like. Often people will reply as if perhaps all I am interested in is whether something traumatic or difficult happened to them: 'My childhood was fine, there's nothing to report.' The thing is that there is always something to report, whether traumatic or not. I'm curious about the feel of someone's family, the way they did things, the way they talked about things (or didn't), the way they resolved things or didn't, what relationships looked like, what their attitudes were to things. Because all of these will end up as part of the mix that a couple have to manage between them in their own relationship. Thinking about the different aspects of culture that a couple bring into the relationship, whether that of their family or of the broader culture that their family was part of, is something that can really help couples get to know and understand each other better.

Where issues about these differences flare up or show themselves (even in different attitudes about how to do the washing-up), there is an opportunity for learning about each other (and yourself). As part of your relationship, and perhaps starting your own family, if you can manage to stay afloat in this soup of each other's experiences while you get the hang of different aspects of each other, then old hurts can perhaps be repaired and important and intimate knowledge of each other built up. There is also the possibility of a new kind of soup; one that reflects elements of both people's families, bringing together ingredients that are wanted and taking time to identify those which aren't.

When it comes to each individual's wider family, bearing all of this in mind can be of help. You are going to have different ideas about things. You are now linked to members of each other's family in some way and yet you didn't grow up with them. Getting to grips with this is inevitably difficult; you can't expect your partner to feel the way that you do about your family and you may need to bridge the way for one another. This bridge can have different roles – it can help create a route to understanding the other's family; it can also be a bridge that redefines boundaries between you and your respective families; what is important is that you work on these issues together rather than expecting them to be the other person's problem.

What seems to work well for couples in this area

- *Being aware that it can be a very sensitive topic. You may find it easy to complain about your own family but take it very personally when you hear your partner complaining about them.*
- *Taking time to be curious about each other's families, and having an open mind so that you don't assume that your family's way is the 'right way'.*
- *Working together. Leaving your partner to resolve their issues with your family on their own, or telling them to 'get over it' is unlikely to help. Even if you don't have the issues with your family that your partner has, you are still part of helping to find a way to manage the issues better, and if you are avoiding being part of the solution then it may be worth asking if this is an aspect of your family that you too struggle with.*
- *Being clear about what kind of boundaries you are both*

looking for when it comes to involvement with each of your families.

- *Trying not to avoid the issues or pretend they aren't there – they are likely to rear their head. By not avoiding them, potentially difficult areas can be pre-empted, so if, for example, you know that you or your partner struggle with family gatherings, try to think about them before rather than after, and consider how to support each other on the day, perhaps by planning to take time out at some point to check on how you are both doing.*

3

Roles (aka 'You never put the bins out')

Not far behind the washing-up as a hot topic for couples is ... taking out the rubbish. There are different ideas about when the bag needs changing, who is going to take it out of the bin (and who is going to remember to take the dustbins out on the right day). And how much thanks whoever does these things should get are questions that are important in relation to the real-life rubbish itself. At a deeper level these questions are symbolic of the negotiations that are required to work out what needs doing, who does what, and how you both feel about the jobs you have to do in the relationship. Does one of you have to deal with more 'rubbish' than the other? In both cases, real and symbolic, if these questions don't get attended to or thought about, then things can start to smell. We have arguments about the things we have to do because doing all these things is hard work, and there is huge potential for resentments or disappointments.

When couples argue or express irritation to each other about the jobs they're doing, it's their way of flagging up these resentments or disappointments. These are 'arguments we need to have' because no couple can glide easily into a state where everything gets done without negotiations, some difficult, particularly when they have children and the to-do list becomes bigger and harder, and on less sleep (there's more about this subject, specifically in relation to children, in chapter 6). Being in a couple means struggling together with a workload, but without the help of an HR department to review whether the workload is manageable and how everyone feels about it. So couples need to figure this out for themselves. Within this area, money can intensify worries and exacerbate resentments.

I do more than you do (part 1)

The feeling 'I do more than you do' is a core issue that can really get to people about their partner – whether it's a feeling that they're the only one who ever remembers to think about the bin or that they care more about the children getting their homework done or that they take more responsibility for the finances. When people feel that they're doing more than their partner, or that their partner isn't pulling their weight, it can stir up feelings of not being cared for, not being respected, not being thought about. Often it is in the shared domain of the home that these tensions find a stage.

It is a Saturday morning. Leyla is vacuuming loudly, moving things out of her way and telling one of her children that she can't play with him right now as the house needs cleaning. She tells her children to go and tidy their rooms. Her partner Andy, who has been reading the news on his phone, starts to realise that the vacuuming has a special loud feel to it; this is not just vacuuming, it is angry vacuuming. He carries on reading, ignoring the noise, until at one point Leyla comes right up to where he is sitting and he asks her through the noise 'What's all the stress?!'

LEYLA: Does it not occur to you that the house is in a total state?
ANDY: Well no actually, I think it looks fine, and I think it's more important that we have a relaxing morning than worrying about the mess. I'll do it later.

Leyla, fuming, carries on with the job. It turns out that her angry vacuuming is quite effective and she feels quite satisfied with it. She walks into the kitchen where she picks up the plates from breakfast and loads them clashingly into the dishwasher. She then heaves the bin bag out of the bin.

ANDY (shouts from where he is sitting): I can do that later!
LEYLA: But it needs doing now!

Andy doesn't agree that it needs doing now, and feels that if Leyla chooses to spend her Saturday morning cleaning up in a huff then that is her problem. He has had a hard week at work and feels that an hour on the sofa is uncontroversially justified.

Leyla is angry with Andy for the rest of the day and later on, whenever she encounters something messy around the house, it just confirms her angry feelings. Andy is frustrated about the atmosphere in the house and thinks she is overreacting. Not much is said out loud, but the tone between them is very frosty.

Here we have an 'argument' in the area of who does what. Leyla is cross that she is working harder than Andy. But Andy doesn't think that this is work that needs doing. The difference of opinion is actually in defining what needs doing. Both of them have a clear idea of what they think needs doing, with Leyla thinking the house needs to be tidied and the bin emptied, and Andy thinking it doesn't (or at least – not yet).

They could do nothing about this tension and let it rear its head whenever it needs to (probably quite often). Indeed, this way of relating is quite familiar to them – they've both seen their parents have this kind of argument since they were children. It may be manageable for them both to deal with the realities of their responsibilities in this way and to have this kind of tension every weekend. Their children are already used to the feel of this dynamic between their parents and know that 'mum complains about dad not doing enough housework'.

For as long as this argument remains an argument about who is right, then they may not get very far with changing the dynamic between them on this issue. Thinking about what actually might be possible may be more realistic. It may not be possible for them to feel the same about tidiness. It reminds me of a conversation that a friend of mine, Susie, told me she had had with her partner:

MY FRIEND SUSIE: I'm so fed up with tidying up after everyone.

Five Arguments All Couples (Need To) Have

HER PARTNER DAVE: But you love tidying!
MY FRIEND SUSIE: I don't love tidying; I love TIDY!

We all have different capacities for tidiness and mess. Some can bear more than others. Clearly Leyla 'loves tidy' more than Andy does. For some people, things on the floor or washing up in the sink equals chaos whereas for others it's perfectly fine. Some of us can let the bin fill up all the way to the top; some of us feel it needs taking out when it's two-thirds full. Realistically there will be a range of approaches here. So if a couple can see that one of them simply may not have the same capacity for mess as the other, then something of the struggle for 'rightness' on the issue can be given up.

In Leyla's case, to own this may be a painful reality not only about Andy but also about herself; the reality that 'I do more than you do because it matters to me more than it does to you'. If she stays wedded to an expectation that Andy is going to match her capacity for mess (or indeed anything) then she is perhaps going to get stuck being perpetually disappointed.

On Andy's side, the painful reality is that this issue isn't going away, because even if it apparently doesn't matter so much to him whether or not the house is messy, it does matter to Leyla. If he feels that the answer to the situation is for Leyla to feel as he does, he is going be similarly disappointed. He too may have to give up something of his vision in order to move on from this argument.

It's frustrating when we discover that our partners care more (or less) than we do about something, because this means that they will have a different idea of the work involved in relation to it. Our arguments can be an attempt to show our partners how much we care about something and to get them to care as much as we do, and to work as hard as we do at it. But managing to share the space with someone may also mean having to accept the painful reality that they simply don't care as much (or as little) as we do about whatever it is. A conversation that seeks to understand where the other partner is coming from can help create a more sympathetic environment in which to accept these realities.

For example, rather than 'You're so obsessed with tidy', Andy might ask Leyla 'Why is tidy so important to you?' And similarly, Leyla might wonder 'What impact does it have on you that I care so much about things being tidy?' When these things are better understood between them there is less need for them to be conveyed angrily and perhaps a better chance of getting help from the other.

If we think of this argument as one potentially about 'what is the work that needs doing' then there may be more room for negotiation. For example, Leyla may find that if she modifies her idea that the work that needs doing is 'everything being tidied up right now' and changes it to 'everything being tidied up at some point over the weekend' then she may have a more realistic chance of getting some help.

This example might seem a bit of a gender stereotype, with Andy, the man, being the one who doesn't care as much about mess as his female partner. It's true that I have seen a lot of women in my consulting room complaining that their male partners don't pull their weight domestically. However, I have seen it the other way too, in lots of heterosexual couples where the man asks his female partner to be tidier (shout out here to my patient husband) and in same-sex couples where there are plenty of arguments about mess and housework. It seems to me to be about the internal vision each person has about something and to what extent they can give some of this up for the sake of incorporating that of the other. This could of course apply to themes other than housework, but because the state of our home is such a shared experience, these tensions often get expressed in this domain. If we physically live together, managing these is likely to involve both people having to give up some of their individual visions about how their home is going to run or look or how much work is going to be involved (a good symbol of the general problem of being in a relationship!).

Ideas for reflection
- *What expectations do you have about how messy or tidy or clean your living space should be?*
- *What are your partner's expectations?*
- *Where do you think these expectations come from?*
- *How do you communicate with each other about housework?*
- *Does it tend to be productive?*
- *How do you feel the housework is shared out between you? Is it clear who is responsible for what?*

I do more than you (part 2 – I really do)
You might say – 'this is all very well that we have to come to terms with each other's different visions of what the

work is that needs doing, but I actually really do think I do more than my fair share in my relationship, and if I don't take the rubbish out or earn the money or [insert whatever work you feel you do more of] then no one will.' Sometimes I see couples where one of them feels at their wit's end in this kind of position, feeling isolated and over-burdened and without support from their partner. Coming to couple therapy is sometimes their last resort, a way to get their partner to hear how desperately unfair they feel the situation is.

Frank and Cinzia were struggling. Both worked in restaurants and had long shifts, which was particularly hard as they were often working at different times. Frank had arranged for them to come to therapy. He said that he was at a crisis point. He complained that even though they both had similar working hours, it was he who took care of the house, who did the shopping, who managed their bills, who fed the cat. When Cinzia had a lie-in if they had a shared day off, while Frank got up to do chores, Frank found it hugely provocative. Frank had told Cinzia that he was thinking of ending the relationship because he felt that he was getting nothing out of it, only putting in.

I only saw them a few times but the pattern of the sessions was similar. Frank would become very angry with Cinzia about what he felt was the unfair division of labour and Cinzia would refuse to engage with him, saying that Frank's words were cruel and unfair, and that this wasn't a fair reflection of the situation. The sessions with me were very tense and it wasn't a surprise to me when after a few appointments Frank emailed to say that they had decided not to continue with the therapy as they had decided to split up. He said that the sessions hadn't been of help to them.

I really didn't have a chance to understand what was going on between them. It was clear that their external circumstances in relation to their jobs was highly pressured. What seemed to be missing was a chance to have any kind of constructive forum about the situation without it becoming defensive. Couple therapy had perhaps been an attempt at making this conversation more constructive but such a conversation didn't seem a possibility for them.

While there may have been many aspects to their difficulties, having a constructive setting in which to talk about feelings about the work a couple feel they are each doing for the relationship is crucial. I mean a kind of space in which they can acknowledge their feelings about each other's roles and think about the implications of those roles for their relationship. It's what I think of as a necessary 'HR function' in a couple. Just as employees start their jobs with contracts, and then over time have opportunities (at least you hope they do, in a well-managed organisation) to review their workloads, express any concerns or hopes or difficult aspects about their jobs, or possibly renegotiate their contracts, so in a relationship it can be important to find ways to think about what the 'contract' is between two people – what is the understanding of who is going to do what – and on an ongoing basis to review the way that the 'labour' gets shared.

Creating this 'HR function' within a relationship ties in with ideas from chapter 1 about communicating. It might mean a conversation that spells out and reviews who is doing what. Some people feel that they are doing a workload that is huge but which the other person doesn't even see because it is less quantifiable,* less obvious or doesn't bring in money. It might be about the jobs you would sometimes like to do on your own and would sometimes rather your partner didn't get involved in. It might mean having the space to speak about how hard you find the responsibilities you seem to have, or having the space to say that you envy the other person their different position. It might mean finding a way to speak about your different ambitions and aspirations and to think together about the implications of these on the relationship. A very typical situation here is where one person is hugely involved with their job and is working all hours. Now this may be a set-up that actually works for both people in the relationship, giving them a distance from each other that they need; but it may create a loss in connection and threaten the relationship. Being able to think together about what this means for them and finding a way to acknowledge and address the difficulties it poses may be essential to keeping a sense of connectedness alive.

When Leyla and Andy have an argument about the housework in the way that we saw earlier, we might wonder if it is a warning sign indicating that it would be helpful to have this HR-type of conversation. If, when they've cooled off from their angry feelings, they can revisit the issue then there might be an opportunity to get to know something important about each other.

---

*I am going to give these less quantifiable jobs a little moment of their own later.

Five Arguments All Couples (Need To) Have

ANDY: It seems like you were really angry about the housework yesterday. Are you okay? Is this just about how messy the house is or is there more to it?

LEYLA: Actually I am feeling quite down about my situation. I feel fed up with the relentlessness of dealing with the house and overwhelmed by managing work and home. I envy you being able to not have to think about it as much as me because you are out at work full-time. I also feel like you don't respect me when you don't pick up your stuff.

This conversation could, as it so often does, get competitive. Andy could feel that he needs to say all the things he does too: 'It's not like I don't do anything.' This could leave them both unsatisfied. with neither of them feeling that the work they do is acknowledged.

Alternatively, if Andy can manage to hear this without feeling attacked (and Leyla is helping with this by talking about how she is feeling rather than by saying how dreadful he is) then there is quite a lot for him to learn about where Leyla is coming from.

ANDY: Wow, okay, there's quite a lot for me to think about in that.

(There may be aspects for Leyla to understand about Andy's experience too.)

LEYLA: What about you? Is everything okay?

ANDY: Actually when I get home at the end of the week

I'm exhausted. I realise that that is frustrating for you but at the moment I don't have much in the tank and I feel like I've had people demanding things from me all week. It's not meant to be personal to you; it's just that I really need to recharge myself. You're much more likely to get a better response out of me if I can just have a bit of quiet time to myself.

In this case, the argument they've had helps signpost and clarify important feelings about their different roles that seem to need airing. Leyla is finally able to identify that she feels a bit overwhelmed and even that she isn't feeling cared for. This isn't just about the mess. The response from Andy is showing some of his more fragile feelings (which aren't so obvious when he is on the defensive) and this gives Leyla more chance to orient herself with how to get a better response out of him if she wants his help with the housework.

Ideas for reflection
- *How do you feel about the division of labour in your relationship?*
- *Do you feel able to discuss the implications of your different roles?*
- *Would you like more acknowledgement for the role you do?*
- *Do you acknowledge what your partner does?*

Pressures on who does what
Sometimes the 'contract' about who does what in the relationship has to change, and this can create pressure

and tension. At this point there may be tension that didn't previously exist and this may be a sign that the question of 'who does what' needs tending to.

This was an issue for so many couples in lockdown – me included, as I negotiated with my husband to build in writing time for this book within the chaotic pressure cooker that was working from home, home-schooling and keeping the show on the road. Lockdown created a situation in which families urgently had to deal with more work – for some there were more domestic duties and the responsibilities required in home-schooling children, for others the intense pressures of frontline essential work or caring. I worked in a lockdown programme to support couples, and the pressure of the situation clearly created resentments within relationships where one person felt that they were doing more work than the other or where they felt that jobs that used to be theirs autonomously now seemed to be in a shared domain. At this point couples needed to find a way to think quickly and flexibly with one another and to divide up the work that needed doing. While the situation was intense and extraordinary, it seemed to me to symbolise the flexibility and co-operative mindset that is required to be able to deal with issues around the division of labour. When couples were able to review the situation with each other, not only to work out who was doing what, but also to acknowledge and appreciate the work their partner was doing, it took the heat out of the issue and helped them to feel that they were working together, however hard it was.

Lockdown was an extreme example of this, but life presents many potential changes to a contract between partners and so needs revisiting. It may be a brief period of change (for example one person is away, or has a particularly busy work schedule) or perhaps something less temporary – illness or a change in employment or an increase in caring responsibilities. Whatever the situation, tensions can easily build around the change and the rejigging of responsibilities, which may be a sign that the feelings around the change need to be visited. The moment when children come along clearly requires a review of the way the workload is shared, but more of that in chapter 6.

You just take me for granted

I have often worked with couples where resentments about the responsibilities they feel they have in the relationship have built up over the years to the point where these have corroded it, sometimes to the point of ending it. The daily things can add up here. Doing the housework every day without acknowledgement, shouldering the financial responsibility without feeling that it is appreciated, being the one who always organises things without it ever being questioned – all this can work for some people but it can also build up resentments that get in the way of couples feeling loving towards one another.

Ruth (whom we also met in chapter 1) spoke of her feelings about having been in a traditional set-up where her husband Ray went out to work and she stayed at home with the children. She said that she felt that her role as home-maker had always been taken for granted. She felt that she and Ray had never found a way to show appreciation for each other's roles. She said, 'I think it is my generation. We did the traditional roles required of us and didn't think that it was necessary to comment on them. It's only now I'm older that I realise that I was longing for more appreciation than I asked for. We didn't have any kind of language for this sort of conversation.'

Work that seems to be required in this area is recognition for the jobs that we do. It isn't that you necessarily want your partner to do the jobs you do, but you want recognition for doing them. Even if it is written in stone that your partner puts the bins out every Monday, and that this has been negotiated very clearly between you and doesn't need revisiting every week, it doesn't mean that it never has to be acknowledged. When I see this sharing of workload going well between couples, it's not only that it goes smoothly, it's also that there are expressions of gratitude, on an ongoing basis, between them, even for the things that are hard to quantify.

Why are you expecting me to do that?

Ruth referred to the culture she had been brought up in and how that had played out in the work she did in her relationship. In the mix of all the ideas that we bring to our relationships about who does what are the ideas and models from the cultures we've grown up in, both in our families and in the wider culture, about how jobs get shared out and how negotiations about these things happen (or don't). Many of the couples I work with are sharing the workload differently from how their parents did. Without the more traditional template governing how things are done, the possibilities are wider, and so is the need for conversations and negotiations. These 'arguments' are potentially so rich, as families define for themselves the way in which they want to set up the division of labour. But where I often see issues is where there is a divergence between the workload that they think they've set up and the realities of how it operates in practice. One striking study after the first lockdown showed how, in heterosexual couples, women tended to be doing more childcare and more housework than men, even when both were working full-time. It didn't say how women were feeling about this, but I think I can guess. Tensions can really build up when one partner in a couple feels they are doing a particular job but are also saddled with other jobs that they hadn't signed up for. As one of my friends said to me – 'if we don't keep talking about how we are trying to do it differently from our parents then we just fall back into doing it their way, but with a whole lot more resentment'. It points again to this need to keep in touch with how both people are feeling about the work they are doing in the relationship (or about the work they feel their partner isn't doing). This creates the possibility of adjustments being made, or of greater acknowledgement about the way in which things are set up.

The templates we've grown up with can operate at other levels. Ty and Kim were getting on really badly about the responsibilities they felt they both had in the relationship, often giving a sense that they were competing about who had the harder time, whether with work, childcare responsibilities or housework. The situation was eroding goodwill between them.

Hearing about their backgrounds gave some context to the intense feelings they seemed to be struggling with.

Ty felt he had always been someone who was responsible for looking out for people. His parents had divorced acrimoniously when he was thirteen, and his parents had turned to him to look out both for his younger sister and for each of them following the divorce. He very much felt he had been expected to be 'the man of the house' for his mum. Kim too had had responsibilities growing up within her family; she was eight years older than her twin sisters and had always helped look after them. Before they had children Ty and Kim had felt relatively independent and free in their relationship, but now the reality of family life was touching upon old frustrations they might have had about the 'workloads' they had as children. In order to attend to their current frustrations with each other, it was a help to understand that this was a sensitive issue for both of them.

Money issues

Problems in this area of sharing out work often relate to a wish to feel valued. It isn't a surprise, then, that arguments about money provide fertile ground for playing out some of the issues involved. When I worked as a divorce lawyer it was very common to hear the frustration of people who felt that on divorce they were entitled to more money than their partner because they had been the one to earn it or had earned more of it (the law – thankfully – doesn't generally agree with this line of thought!). It exposed how the roles in a relationship can be valued differently by the people in it.

Where there are serious money concerns, issues in this area will be intensified, and it may be hard for couples to think about much else other than how to survive. The pressures and worries of being in this sort of situation will dominate and may intensify conflicts. But even where concerns about money aren't about day-to-day survival they can be a source of conflict, often flaring up as an issue about who has responsibility for what in the relationship.

Marie and Sunil were in their late twenties and had been together for about eighteen months. Sunil had suggested that Marie move in with him as the lease on her flat was up and his flatmate had recently moved out. They were both really excited and happy to take this next step. They had talked briefly about how it would work in terms of finances, with Marie contributing to half the rent but none of the bills unless her earnings increased. Things had been going smoothly until they had an argument one day about money. It had started from something small – Marie hadn't had her wallet on her when they were out getting coffee and Sunil had gone quiet and sulky after he had paid. When they got home and Marie had asked him what was wrong, it had come out that Sunil felt that he was always the one thinking about money and that Marie seemed to have her head in the clouds about it. He felt as if he was always paying for things. Marie was horrified that the simple act of leaving her wallet behind could have made him jump to this conclusion. But then it all came out – he was feeling nervous that he was taking on more financial responsibility than her and this was making their relationship feel quite serious. She said that she would never dream of taking advantage of him but that she found it hard to bring up money as a subject – it wasn't something that had been talked about much in her family and she felt uncomfortable acknowledging that she was relying on him to pay the bills.

The issue of money seemed to be an argument this couple needed to have about the different responsibilities in the relationship. The small incident around the coffee alerted them to deeper concerns that needed tending to, not only about who was paying for things but about how much they could at this point trust or rely on each other. It also flagged up different attitudes to money, for example that Marie might not find it easy to talk about. Everyone has their own particular relationship and set of experiences relating to money. These will affect how they talk about it, what hopes or expectations they might have, what fears about not having it or having it, how they feel about spending it, or how comfortable they feel about running up debt. The ways in which couples clash about these issues may be the hard but inevitable route to learning about each other in this essential area and mapping their different ideas.

In this situation, the fact was that Sunil could afford something that Marie could not, and the argument they had could also be seen as a way of struggling with this reality. For many couples there is no getting away from the reality that one of them has an earning capacity that the other doesn't and they may feel stuck in a position that they wouldn't necessarily have chosen but that is required in order to pay the bills. When this comes up with couples I work with, what seems to help is for the frustrations and disappointments about this situation to be aired between them rather than avoided as a no-go zone.

It's also important to focus on any issues of the power

dynamics that might be created by one person earning more than the other. Might Marie, for example, feel she has less say about what they do as a couple if she feels that Sunil is always paying for things? Where might the feelings about this come out if she doesn't express them? How might Sunil feel about this? What does being financially dependent on someone else mean for the relationship? Often these issues can rear their head when there is a change in the way finances are set up. For example, when a couple have a baby and one of them reduces their work in order to look after it, there may be real feelings about dependency and loss of power. Making space in the relationship to reflect on this can be hugely important.

Ideas for reflection
- *How comfortable do you feel talking about money?*
- *How was money talked about in your family?*
- *Did you grow up with particular family ideas or worries about money?*
- *Does one of you earn more than the other and if so what does this mean to you?*

Why do you have to be such a worrier/Why is it my job to get us to the airport on time?

I've talked about the kinds of roles people have as well as ideas about workloads, and whether the issues are about housework, dealing with the finances, or going out and earning money. But there are other, sometimes more subtle, roles that couples end up dividing between them, perhaps without even realising it.

For example, some couples find that one of them worries more and one is more relaxed. Or perhaps one is a planner while the other tends to go along with whatever plans are made. Sometimes people feel that they have to take on being the grown-up in the relationship. The one who has to say 'it's time for us to go now' at the end of the evening. Or the one who says 'we can't afford that'. One may feel that they are the 'fixer' and the other is more vulnerable. One of you may be reading this book and feel that you do the thinking about your relationship or about your family while your partner doesn't. Sometimes the sharing out of these different roles can be seen following a separation or bereavement, where there is a need for someone to take back or step up to a role that had been their partner's.

These different approaches, these different areas of responsibility or competence can work in a complementary way, and are perhaps part of what attracts us to our partners. Couples can be good at spreading out these kind of things between them – sometimes without even realising that that's what they are doing. Some couples over time find an equilibrium, a system maintained between them that isn't problematic for either of them.

But just as there are feelings about 'I do too much of this [housework] [childcare] [earning],' so there can be feelings of 'I do too much of this [worrying] [planning] [organising] [initiating fun]', or 'why is it me who has to make sure we get to the airport on time'. Because these roles are less concrete, less obvious, harder to quantify, then it can be harder to notice them or talk with each other about them.

Sam and Vaz are a typical example of this (and money found its way into this situation too). Sam was furious with Vaz when he found out that Vaz had booked a night away for the two of them at a hotel. Vaz couldn't believe that Sam was having such a bad reaction to it.

VAZ : Nothing I can do is right! I try and do something nice and you still don't appreciate me!

SAM: Well, you never think about the cost of things do you? You know we can't afford this. And who's going to look after the kids?

VAZ: I just thought we needed it! You're so boring, why are you never up for some fun any more?

SAM: I don't want to be the one who says no to all the fun. It's not like I don't want to have fun. But this feels really extravagant and I've no idea how we will find a babysitter in time.

The conflict here between them flags up something important – namely how they feel they are stuck in different places and therefore find it hard to make joint decisions about things. Sam feels that he has to be the dampener, the one who worries about money, whereas Vaz seems to have ended up on the other end of the spectrum looking as if he's the only one who cares about fun and spontaneity.

Seeing this argument as a warning light about how their different roles need looking at could provide a useful opportunity for them to try to develop the situation.

SAM: You know I do like thinking about having fun

too. I just don't trust you to think about all the serious stuff.

In order for Sam to be able to get out of the place in which he feels stuck, he is going to have to build up trust in a way that it is safe for him to do. This requires Vaz to engage with Sam's need to trust him.

VAZ: But how can I get you to trust me?
SAM: I don't know. I guess I have this idea that you just don't think about the serious aspects of things, you just leave it to me.
VAZ: Well yes I think I probably do but you're just better at it!
SAM: Well, I'm fed up of being stuck with that job.

Vaz has here acknowledged that he behaved in the way he did because he knows that Sam has the job of thinking about the 'serious aspects'. If this argument can result in both being ready to change a dynamic where one of them is fed up, then perhaps something helpful can develop.

In a situation where one of you feels stuck, changing that dynamic will first need both of you to acknowledge what is happening. It will take a bit of a shift between the two of you. One of you may have to relinquish a role that has felt comfortable and one may have to step up to a role that hasn't. Finding a way to speak to each other about the difficulties of shifting role can help.

SAM: It is really hard for me to trust you. It doesn't come naturally. It would help me if we could talk more about money, for example, so that I can see you are engaging with our situation.

VAZ: I tend to shy away from those conversations as I worry that you'll pick me up on not being as up to speed as you but if you can bear with me I am totally up for trying.

Here Vaz is showing a wish to be more engaged with money, a shift which means that Sam has an opportunity to hand over some of the responsibility. This not only requires action from Vaz but also from Sam, as he has to dare to let him take it on, which may take some patience and frustration on Sam's part as Vaz 'gets up to speed'.

This happens often. You might find that a person who appears to be the worrier or the anxious one in the relationship is carrying that role for both people. Sometimes we let our partners take the roles we aren't so comfortable with, or the roles in which we don't feel competent. And sometimes we take roles that feel familiar or important to us. For example we might end up in a worrying role, or in a role of responsibility if that's what we're used to, or if we've grown up feeling that other people weren't worrying on our behalf.

At the same time we have a lot to learn by being alongside someone who is different from us, or who is competent in an area in which we don't feel competent. This is how couples can help one another to come out of their comfort zones.

I like to think of seesaws. Where couples get frustrated about being stuck in their particular roles, it might look like a seesaw that has ground to a halt, with one person stuck in one place and one stuck in the other. To get it going again, both are going to have to shift a bit, and one may have to do more moving, or jump-starting. Like Sam and Vaz – where Sam is going to have to step back and Vaz is going to have to step up.

Sometimes this shift in roles isn't possible; sometimes it may be that one of you is keen to make such a shift but the other one isn't. The reality may mean that this is a turning point and it may be that there is some mourning to be done about what isn't possible. For example, if Sam were to let himself trust Vaz more but is then repeatedly let down, he would need to work out how much this mattered to him. Or if one of you always has to take responsibility for getting to places on time, maybe that is something that can be known about in the relationship as an unwanted, but appreciated, role – and that, it turn, will make it easier to manage the frustration of having to keep doing it. The rows in this area can be teething problems early on in a relationship as it becomes apparent that certain jobs need to be taken on. But as things settle down, this can become manageable, however disappointing this might be to the one who takes on an unwanted role.

Rick and Sadie argued because Rick realised that if he didn't point out what time it was, Sadie would never be ready to leave. This wasn't ever something he'd had to deal with before – he found it easy to get to places on time, and now he was in a relationship with someone who struggled with this. There was a familiar pattern as they argued about it, with Rick repeatedly trying to get Sadie to be better at tuning in to what time it was and Sadie seemingly unable to change. Over time, he started to accept how difficult it was for her to do things differently. This wasn't a situation he would have chosen, but it seemed easier to modify things on his side – making sure that they built in even more time than he would have thought they needed. What made it easier was Sadie seeing that this was how she was; it wasn't something she'd had to face before, but now that Rick kept pointing it out she became more aware of the impact it had on him, even if, despite trying, she seemed to be unable to change. The effort she put into acknowledging the impact she had was helpful.

There can be different roles within a relationship that feel really hard to resolve, for example where one person has a problem with alcohol and their partner feels that they are always on edge or having to pick up the pieces. Or where one person in the relationship is depressed and their partner feels overwhelmed with caring for them. In polarised situations like this, professional support may help couples think about what these different roles mean for them and how to find a way forward together.

Ideas for reflection
- *Do you feel there are subtle roles in the relationship that you or your partner carry?*
- *Are they spoken or unspoken?*
- *Do they relate to roles you've carried before?*
- *Do you feel comfortable with them?*

What about the washing-up?
If I was considering the issues in this chapter and thinking about Evie and Ashley's arguments about the washing-up (or Leyla's noisy loading of the dishwasher) I'd be

thinking about how the washing-up provides such a ripe opportunity for revealing tensions and resentments about workloads in the relationship, and wondering things such as:

- Does this argument about the washing-up allude to issues that need addressing here in terms of the couples' workloads?
- What possibility or flexibility is there here for the couple to give up their vision of how things should be done?
- What messages from family and society are getting into the mix here?
- Is there an unspoken deal between them about how they share things out that needs reviewing? Is Evie the one who takes responsibility for things while Ashley sits back? Are they both a part of perpetuating this dynamic?
- To put it rather obviously – is one of them doing far more washing-up/dishwasher loading than the other and what are the feelings about that?

Unacknowledged labour
While washing-up stares you in the face, there are some jobs that need doing that aren't so obvious. Because I sometimes hear how these jobs are creating frustrations, I'm going to give them a special paragraph of their own.

Examples of jobs that often don't get enough acknowledgement in a relationship:

- Worrying about money/the future/health.

- Thinking about what's going on in your relationship.
- Attending to family members who are sad or upset.
- Investing in relationships – family members.
- Investing in relationships – networks, e.g. school community.
- Planning journeys or trips.
- Washing – sorting it into colours, doing it, folding it, putting it away. Oh, and reuniting socks.
- Planning social lives.
- Changing light bulbs.
- Car maintenance/tax.
- Making GP or dentist or vet appointments, arranging prescriptions and medication, administering medication – anything in the medical area.
- Remembering/organising birthdays or writing thank-you letters.
- Knowing where things live in your home/putting things back in the place they live/finding places for things to live.
- Clearing out children's clothes that have been grown out of (or indeed any kind of clearing out).
- Making sure whatever needs taking into school is taken into school (and that it comes home again).
- Buying cleaning products, toiletries, toilet roll.
- Filling up the car with fuel.

Some of these may seem like small things, and you may think: how can we acknowledge all of this between us? Surely we won't have time to ever do anything else? But when someone is doing lots of these jobs and isn't getting acknowledgement for them, then they can all add up and create resentment.

Idea for reflection
- *Are there any jobs you would like to add to this list?! This may be their moment in the limelight.*

Summing up

Sharing space with a partner means sharing out all the jobs that need to be done to look after the space, whether physical jobs like tidying up or earning money, or making sure that what needs to be worried about gets worried about. When this is going well there can be real enjoyment from a sense of collaboration and teamwork. As we observe ourselves in our relationships and see how we divide things up (or deal with the frustrations of how things are divided up) we also have the chance to understand more about ourselves – about the roles we are drawn to take on, the ones we avoid, the ones we are more comfortable with letting our partners do (or the ones we aren't comfortable with letting them do).

But the route into working out who does what is rarely smooth. There may be different ideas about what work actually needs doing, and different expectations about who is going to do what (and then the things that need doing change and the whole thing needs re-evaluating). Sometimes it's a bit of a struggle as we try to claim the roles we want or try to fend off the roles we don't want; and just when it settles, life changes and all needs renegotiating. Feelings about the division of labour (and the often difficult realities involved in having to take on responsibilities that are challenging, or not what we imagined or hoped they would be) can often tip into feelings of unfairness and resentment. These feelings can often be really toxic to a relationship unless they are actively addressed. There is work to do about what we each do in the relationship, just to add to the to-do list.

What seems to work well for couples in this area

- *Showing appreciation of what you each do really matters.*
- *Not making assumptions about what your partner's workload involves.*
- *Not expecting your partner to mind-read and do the things that you think need doing – this links in with communicating well to each other about what these are.*
- *Support networks matter – being able to let off steam with friends about the jobs you end up doing in your relationships.*
- *Being up for having a go at something that you don't normally do.*
- *Checking in regularly on how you are both feeling about workloads.*
- *Understanding that you really may have different ideas of what counts as something that needs clearing up.*
- *Acknowledging the impact you might have of finding a particular role or responsibility really difficult.*

4

Comings and goings (aka 'Why are you always on your phone? or, can you just give me some space?')

I'm looking round a restaurant and noticing different couples. Some of them are facing and talking to each other. One girl is sitting on her boyfriend's lap. One couple are eating together in silence. Quite a few of them are on phones – some with just one person on a phone, some with both of them. One person gets up to leave and says goodbye to the person they're with.

These different set-ups strike me as being a snapshot of the different places or states of mind we might move between in our couple relationships. Of course there's the moving into a relationship, the getting together (and every couple may have a different idea of what this togetherness looks like), but then within a relationship there are different states of closeness and connectedness between two people. Sometimes we share things with each other, sometimes we are together physically but mentally somewhere else, sometimes one person is mentally somewhere else but with their partner wishing that they could be thinking more about them, sometimes we are physically apart but thinking of each other (or not). There can be quite a lot of tension in this area as we discover the different ideas we each have about what distance we want or can bear from one another (physically or mentally), about how much autonomy we have, and what of ourselves we want to or can bear to share with the other.

So in this chapter I'm going to look at some of these different states, these 'comings and goings' that couples may struggle with (and I'll also talk quite a lot about phones ...).

Why are you always on your phone?

Phones are a major theme of this chapter, perhaps because they are a way in which, while we are physically with our partners, we are doing something else with someone or something else, and are therefore creating a kind of distance. As one man said to me, 'There are three of us in this relationship – me, my partner and her phone.' The tensions around each other's phones can hit some raw nerves. First – how do we feel when our partners aren't available to us? When they aren't sharing themselves with us? And second – how do we feel if our partners are enjoying something that we aren't part of?

Eric and Dani often rowed about Dani being on her phone. The row would go something like this:

ERIC: I wish you'd just get off your phone. You've been on it all morning.

DANI: What's the big deal? It's not like we are doing

anything else. Why do you always get so cross about this?

ERIC: (Silent and furious)

DANI: I'm literally doing stuff that I need to do! I'm messaging my sister and if I don't buy the train ticket now it's going to be twice as expensive tomorrow. Why are you always on my case?!

When they row like this, it becomes a very polarised kind of exchange – with Eric sticking to the 'you're always on your phone' complaint and Dani holding to the 'what is your problem?' position. How can anyone argue with the idea of a cheaper train ticket?!

Well, if we thought about it another way, we might wonder what goes through Eric's mind when he feels that Dani is somewhere else. Underneath the silent huff there may be some more vulnerable feelings to hear about and for he and Dani to discover. It may take a bit of work to get these known.

ERIC: I wish you'd get off your phone. I know you want to be on it but I feel a bit left on my own here. I feel like you're somewhere else. Or maybe you don't think I'm very interesting.

DANI: What?! Where on earth has that come from??!! Why would you feel that?

There's a huge gap here between Eric's experience of Dani doing something else and what Dani's experience is. For Eric, it seems to feel quite threatening.

Dani could go down the route of 'you're massively

overreacting'. But if they could both take a moment to contemplate that this is a sensitive area for Eric, then it may make more sense to be curious about what goes on for Eric as Dani 'comes and goes'. If I were working with them and this was an issue that came up repeatedly, I'd want to ask Eric what his experience was growing up in terms of his caregivers coming and going, about how much he felt he was safe and in their minds. What if it was normal for him to feel that he was not really in the minds of his parents as a child? What if this situation with Dani hit on those nerves?

Understanding this wouldn't need to mean that Dani could never go on her phone again! But it would mean that Dani and Eric could be more aware of it with each other and could work at keeping a sense of feeling connected when they are getting on with different things.

The comings and goings between thinking about something else and giving someone our full attention are natural tides in our relationships. We couldn't possibly give someone our full attention the whole time nor ignore them the whole time but these movements can wash up unexpected emotions and expose unknown sensitivities to which we each need to find ways to respond.

There is another potential tension. When Dani says 'Why are you always on my case?' it may be a way of saying that she really feels intruded upon. Eric needs to know that Dani might find it hard when he reacts in the way he does. The balance between autonomy and togetherness here is a tension with which they are going to have to grapple.

Given the role our phones play in our lives, it's quite

difficult to avoid having to negotiate together over how we use them. We talk about how we need to set appropriate boundaries for the way in which children use their phones and screens but these may also need attending to in a couple. Thinking about when it might be acceptable (or not) for one of you to be on your phone (in your bedroom, when you're out doing something as a couple, when you're eating?) may need to be gone into together. When it comes to someone having to use their phone for work this can be really tricky, with one person feeling frustrated that their partner is unavailable to them (and 'always on their phone') and the other feeling that they have no choice but to be at the mercy of incoming work. However, if this issue causes upset or frustration (as it often does) it may need looking at. Are there ways to limit the impact, for example by ring-fencing times where work doesn't intrude? Can both their feelings about the situation (even if it can't be changed) at least be aired between them in order to be in a better position to work out how important this issue is to them? This links into ideas from the previous chapter.

Ideas for reflection

- *Do you have any ground rules about phones? Do you think you need any?*
- *Do you have a reaction to your partner being on their phone? Are there different times or situations where it feels harder?*
- *Does the idea of someone not being available to you touch any particular nerve?*

The FOMO factor

Some of what Eric has to manage is the idea that Dani is doing something that he isn't part of. This may be easier for some people than for others, and it can be hard for us to understand that a partner has different feelings from our own about not being part of something.

Ingrid and Francesca were a couple in their thirties who had been together for three years. They came to therapy because they kept arguing about friends of Francesca's whom she'd known from before they were together, including Francesca's ex-girlfriend. Ingrid found it hard when Francesca went out for an evening with these friends, and struggled with Francesca messaging them in advance of going out and then messaging them afterwards. The day after such an evening, she and Ingrid would tend to have an argument. Ingrid would typically give Francesca the cold shoulder for a few days and Francesca would feel unfairly treated and unnecessarily controlled by Ingrid, leading to conversations such as this:

INGRID: I just don't see why you have to go out with them so often.

FRANCESCA: Well why not – you get to have a quiet night in, which you love, and I get to go out and have a fun night out, which I love. Everyone's a winner.

INGRID: It's not as simple as that. You don't get it – you're only thinking about you here!

FRANCESCA: Hang on – you've been invited, but you never want to come.

INGRID: Well no, I don't, because I don't want to

spend an evening with people I don't know or like.

FRANCESCA: Not even for me?

INGRID: No, and anyway, I know you don't want me there.

These conversations never seemed to get them anywhere. The atmosphere between them would slowly thaw, until it happened again. After one particularly angry argument they decided to see if it was something they could get help with. They were both desperate to try to change something of the groundhog day quality of this row, which happened every time Francesca went out.

Ingrid owned up to some very fragile feelings about the distance between them on these nights out. She explained to Francesca how insecure it made her feel, which Francesca heard as a criticism. Francesca then slowly began to hear it in a different way, that actually this was an expression not of criticism of her but one of vulnerability on Ingrid's part – something very raw for Ingrid about feeling excluded and left behind. Some of this related to Ingrid's own story. She hadn't found it easy to make friends at school and trust didn't come easily to her. Francesca knew this about her but didn't realise how her going out could stir up these feelings.

Knowing this meant that Francesca could be a bit more tactful about going out. Francesca admitted that she worried that if she acknowledged that she was going out or showed that she knew it was hard for Ingrid that somehow she would be indulging Ingrid. But in fact when she was a bit more tactful about it, Ingrid felt more at ease. Ingrid felt

Francesca was thinking about her, and therefore didn't feel so abandoned. Although there was physical space between them, they felt more connected and therefore better able to manage the distance between them.

Surprisingly, something else emerged. With Ingrid being less apparently 'needy' about the issue, some of Francesca's own neediness had space to emerge. She described to Ingrid how the situation could make her feel nervous too, and part of why she felt she had to always go out was because she was worried she would be excluded from the group if she didn't. It became clear that there were more shared sensitivities about this issue than had originally appeared.

The tensions in this area can leave each person feeling that the other one is 'only thinking of themselves'. But if a couple can signal more actively that they are thinking about each other and taking the other into account, this allows more room for their differences to be managed and creates a feeling that things are being negotiated within the relationship rather than outside it.

This example brings out some of the insecurities that can be stirred up by socialising (and more of that in a bit when it comes to social media). But there may be tensions that are less about insecurity and more about different enjoyment levels when socialising. Quite often one person in a couple might be more extrovert than the other and wants to be out mixing with people, while their partner needs something less socially demanding. This is not likely to be a smooth ride for two people as they figure out a way to tend to their different needs, but the clash of ideas will offer them the potential to learn more about each other's social capacities and to work out what is and isn't possible. This may mean both of them having to give up some of their commitment to going out with friends or staying in quietly, but, as with so many of the differences in this book, this is yet another that we can't expect to get sorted from day one. However, the more aware we can become of these differences and capacities, the more we can try to find arrangements that work for both people. It may make a difference if instead of instantly agreeing to or turning down arrangements, a couple can get better at conferring with each other about it. This can be a shift. There can be pressures against it from old friends used to having someone available to them all the time if that person now has to check with their partner. But it is indicative of the shift from being single to being in a couple that these things now need to be thought about from the relationship's perspective.

Ideas for reflection
- *How sensitive are you to being left out of things? How about your partner?*
- *How aware are you of each other's needs (or not) for socialising?*

You're so selfish
Finding space away from the relationship may take negotiation where one person appears to want to go off separately and the other is expressing a wish to be together.

Matthew's job is intense and at the end of the week he wants to go cycling on a Saturday morning to wind down and relax. Cassie, on the other hand, feels that what she really wants to do on a Saturday morning is to spend some time with him to reconnect after a busy week.

Matthew finds this fairly demanding of her, and Cassie feels let down by him. She experiences his bid for doing something separate on his own as selfish.

MATTHEW: I'd really like to go cycling tomorrow morning.

CASSIE: Oh do you have to?

MATTHEW: Why is your initial response always so negative?

CASSIE: It's always about what you want isn't it?!

MATTHEW: I have to ask your permission to do anything in this relationship. I just need a bit of space sometimes.

CASSIE: What are you saying? That you don't want to spend time with me? What about my needs! I'd love to spend some time with you tomorrow morning.

They are left with a sense that only one person's needs can be met here. However, thinking about what the relationship might need could bring things into better focus. Certainly the relationship needs them to find a way through this. It is clear that they are different in this regard. There seems little possibility that Matthew is going to stop being someone who enjoys cycling and Cassie isn't going to stop being someone who likes chatting and being together with her partner.

If they could think about what the relationship needs, it might relieve some of the feeling that this is a competition between the two of them for who gets their way. The relationship is going to *need* them to adjust. They may need to build up confidence that these parts of themselves can have space in the relationship, but simply not all the time. Just because it isn't always convenient for Matthew to go cycling, it doesn't mean that he has to give it up completely. Similarly, just because Cassie can't always have time together chatting with him, it doesn't mean that there isn't room for this in the relationship.

There also seem to be some fears here. Cassie is worried, perhaps, that it is a sign Matthew doesn't want to spend time with her, and Matthew, meanwhile, is worried that she is being too controlling. Finding a better way to communicate about this whole situation could help them build trust in each other.

MATTHEW: How would you feel about me going cycling tomorrow? I know it's not ideal but I could really do with it as I've had such a hard week and I feel like I'll be more available to you if I've had some time to clear my head.

CASSIE: It would be nice to have one of the mornings quietly at home together but I get that you need it so that's fine.

The way they are now talking shows that that they are more in tune with each other, and have more of an idea about what the other one is looking for – which means that they are more able to create something workable.

The tension here is also not just about one of them getting their own way. It is also about the inevitable problem of finding a balance between independence and togetherness. Thinking about it together, in terms of what the relationship might need, can create greater possibilities for independence, and maybe, by going out of the relationship 'independently', something can be brought back into it. If someone is going off independently to do something that may benefit the relationship, then this can be thought of as part of the equation – Matthew going off cycling may be good for his health and mood, which is good for Cassie. These are all difficult trade-offs and it is unrealistic to think that it's going to be smooth every time as couples work out who is going to give up what. But where there can be an ongoing productive conversation about such things there can be space to 'do the trading' and to build up trust that when someone 'gets to do their thing' there will be reciprocation. This can get more complicated if a couple become parents but more of that in Chapter 6.

I need my space

Ben and Muna, a couple in their late fifties, had been in a relationship for ten years. Although it had always worked for them to live separately, they felt that as they got older, the more it made sense to live together and Muna had moved into Ben's place. Although they had been excited about it, the reality was that it was much harder than they had thought it would be. Ben had told Muna that he needed time alone at home at the weekend; that it was too claustrophobic being with each other all the time. He was feeling panicked at their new reality. Muna had taken this badly and felt really upset that what she had imagined was going to be an exciting new chapter seemed not to be going the way she wanted. The feelings were very raw and they had sought therapy for some help.

The different feelings they expressed about moving in together seemed to symbolise some of the deepest longings as well as the deepest concerns that we all have about our relationships: longings to be close and to be cared for by each other, as well as fears about having to give up something of ourselves, whether our ideas or our ways of doing things, or our freedom – fears that could be represented in any of the tensions discussed in the other chapters of this book. When we talk about tensions around comings and goings, about closeness and distance, we might also be thinking about these more subtle longings and fears and how they operate in the relationship.

With Ben, it emerged that growing up he felt that he'd had very little capacity for autonomy. He had grown up in a disciplinarian family where he was expected to do what he was told. It seemed understandable that he might have anxieties about having to give up something of his freedom. These anxieties had been managed in their previous arrangement but now the feelings had been stirred up. Muna, on her side, had had a very painful divorce before she met Ben, and she too was tentative about making more of a commitment, but she hoped to make a better go of things this time round. She worried that his anxieties were a sign that their relationship wasn't strong enough and she was feeling fairly panicked too.

The tensions that these anxieties produced were a consequence of their development as a couple – an argument they needed to have in order to figure out a way of being together. As they got closer to each other, there were some more difficult feelings that needed tending to.

Ben said that if he could feel heard by Muna about his anxieties about her 'coming into his space', then that would help him feel less stifled by the situation. Just because he was saying these things, it didn't mean that the relationship was over – he just needed her to bear with him. What was striking was that as Ben began to relax into the arrangement and to ease off on his requests for time alone, Muna began to feel the need for more space of her own. It seemed that there were shared fears here that had been initially expressed by Ben but that needed thinking about by both of them. It wasn't particularly smooth for this couple as they got to know more about each other's fears, but it seemed essential that they could hang on to the idea that there were things to learn about each other.

This was a particular example of the tensions around distance regulation that can come up every day and that can be important to think about: where are there possibilities for allowing each other the space that might be required? Take cooking. Couples often describe the different set-ups they have around the kitchen. Some like cooking together and helping each other out, some really want to be able to do it their own way and not have interference from their partner (save perhaps for having them clean up afterwards!), some really don't mind, and some may change depending on their mood. Perhaps if the needs for autonomy (or togetherness) can be tended to in some of the small day-to-day things, this can help create a bigger picture that feels more workable.

Ideas for reflection
- *In your relationship, how – if at all – do you express needs for closeness or distance, or for autonomy or togetherness?*
- *Do you take up different positions on this? Does one of you ask for closeness, one for distance?*
- *What does closeness look like to you in a relationship? Is it physical or emotional or both?*
- *What feels like a comfortable distance?*

Why won't you let me look at your phone (or bank account)? Or why do you think you have the right to look at my phone?

When it comes to distance, another area where couples might have different ideas is about what they share with each other, and about what is and isn't deemed private. It might feel perfectly normal for one person to look at their partner's phone but their partner may feel that it's inappropriate or intrusive. Different people are going to have very personal and different thresholds here.

When it comes up as an issue in relation to money I am always curious to hear about it. The way couples manage their money and bank accounts can be an interesting way in to thinking about their feelings about privacy and sharing. Some couples I've worked with have only one joint bank account for all their money; some have an individual bank account but also a joint bank account; some have two individual bank accounts and no sharing of money at all. There is no right answer – different people feel comfortable with different set-ups, but if you each have different ideas about what's appropriate then it's likely that you're going to have to grapple with these ideas between you at some point. These different ways of holding the couple's resources can be symbolic of anxieties and feelings around getting close and about sharing things with each other.

Liam and Monika spoke in therapy about arguments they were having about money and spending. Monika felt that Liam made too many decisions about what to spend money on without asking her and she was worried because they were trying to save. He said it was money that he had earned that had gone into his own personal account and therefore he didn't feel that he should have to check in with her every time he wanted to buy something. He felt she was being intrusive and that she should trust that he wasn't going to overspend. He said he was as serious about saving as she was. She explained that it wasn't a personal criticism of him; but she was someone who worried about money and experiences in her previous relationships meant that this wasn't an area in which she found it easy to be trusting.

It seemed that this issue would need to be a work in progress for them as they built up trust in each other's intentions and possibly in the relationship itself. In order to try to take into account each other's anxieties, they came up with the idea of agreeing a sum of money below which they didn't need to consult one another about spending. Above a certain amount, it would need joint consent. This was something that they would have a go at seeing how it could work for them.

Ideas for reflection

- *What are your ideas about what information can be shared in the relationship?*
- *What are your hopes or worries about sharing information with each other?*
- *How is your money arranged? Is this something you've worked out together? How easy is it for you to discuss it? Do you discuss it regularly or on a case-by-case basis?*

You've crossed a line!

At the heart of some of the problems faced by couples in this chapter is a struggle to find a way between them to manage a third aspect that is beyond them – whether it's someone's phone use or a hobby or a social life. A more contentious third is where a secret affair has been discovered, which then ends the relationship.

But there are some areas where it's less easy for a couple to work out what the deal is or is not between them. What for one partner feels like acceptable behaviour with another person can be for their partner a deal-breaker. Some people may feel that their out-of-work message exchange with a colleague, or their liking of someone on social media, is harmless, where others may feel that this is totally inappropriate. Sometimes it is only 'after the event' that a couple negotiate these boundaries with each other.

Lil and Mike, a retired couple, came to therapy after it emerged that Mike had had quite an intense exchange of messages over a couple of months with a female friend of theirs. Lil had found the messages, and while there was nothing overtly sexual, they were quite personal and she was surprised at the tone she saw – more open, more honest, telling this other person how he was feeling low at the moment and finding retirement quite hard. Lil had been shocked and had felt betrayed. She had asked Mike to leave and he was living at his brother's.

Lil was very clear that Mike had been having what she called an 'emotional affair' in this exchange. Mike pleaded his innocence; that surely he was allowed to open up to a friend, just as Lil had friends to chat to. He said that he had been feeling quite low and that it had been nice to talk about it. He said he found it really hard to find a way to tell Lil about his sadness and that he also hadn't wanted to hurt her or worry her – in a way it just felt safer to talk to someone else about it.

Lil was very suspicious about the whole situation. She said she had a line and that he had crossed it – she wasn't happy with him speaking to their friend in this way. She acknowledged that some people may feel different, but for her this was absolute. If he was feeling bad in himself then he needed to share it with her. He didn't need to worry about hurting her by telling her his feelings – she could manage it. This was how they had found themselves in therapy, where they used the space to talk about some of the difficult feelings that retirement had brought up.

In this case, Lil made it very clear where she wished to draw the line. Mike was prepared to respect her wishes on this, perhaps because she had made it clear to him that he could open up to her. In working through this situation and attending to their feelings about it they had a potential to get closer to each other. But it doesn't always work like that, and sometimes a situation like this can be a deal-breaker. Differences of ideas about what is appropriate with another person/other people can come up and will need attending to.

Ideas for reflection
- *What ideas in your relationship do you have about what is appropriate (and what isn't) in terms of connecting with people, whether that's messaging them, following them on social media, liking them?*

You don't think of me!

Issues around comings and goings touch on sensitive feelings that we may have about being separate from each other and about how we bear that. Ingrid can feel better about Francesca being away when she feels that Francesca is keeping her in mind. Cassie wants to catch up with Matthew after a long week apart. Some may feel easier about their partner having their head down on their phone if their partner acknowledges that that is what they are doing – in effect, saying a mini goodbye before heading off into phone world.

I've heard many couples making complaints in this area – if only she'd think of me when she was out shopping, if only he'd bring me a present, if only he'd message me when he's away for the day. To some people it really matters to know that when they are physically apart they are being thought about. People can feel stuck between wanting their partner to remember them without having to ask and feeling disappointed when their partner doesn't.

Again, it may be that working harder at communicating can ease the situation – 'I know it sounds mad but it means something to me when you buy me the type of sandwich that I like/a present when you're abroad.' It's disappointing to have to resort to the non-telepathic form of communication, but it may get the desired outcome more often.

Sometimes our reactions to being physically apart are surprising.

Kai had been away on a business trip for a couple of weeks. He and his wife Aimee hadn't been in touch much while he was away, but he had been texting her on his way home and they were both really excited to be seeing each other. But things didn't go the way either expected. Aimee was waiting to give him a hug and offered to make him a drink but he asked her to just give him a bit of time to get showered and sort himself out. He said he also had to make one quick call. When he reappeared he went to hug Amy but she gave him a bit of a cold shoulder. 'Shall we have a drink then?' he asked with a smile. 'Oh sorry,' she said, 'I'm busy with something else now.' Kai felt angry with her and walked out. The longed-for 'reunion' had soured.

This can be so confusing. How was it that they could be looking forward to seeing each other so much and then make such a mess of it?

What we might need to think about here are the feelings that had been building. Aimee's sudden coldness was perhaps her way of managing feelings about how hard it had been to be apart and also about the different experiences they'd been having. At the point at which they reunited, some of the difficult feelings hooked themselves on to the situation. Even though rationally Aimee could see that he needed some time to get sorted before he could relax and be with her, the feelings about the separation found a way to show themselves – confusingly for Kai in a way that pushed him away rather than brought him closer. When he took the phone call it was perhaps just too much for Aimee to bear. It might seem irrational to find just one more thing unbearable, but again, it's a bit like Eric and Dani's situation. Sometimes absence and separation can stir up the most childlike feelings. One minute Aimee is an adult, looking forward to seeing her partner, and the next she is grappling with disappointments that have sent her back to feeling more like a child. This is less overreaction and more just human.

In a situation like this, where a 'reunion' hasn't gone so well, a couple might need to try to have a conversation in which they can repair things – a different kind of reunion I suppose. For example, in this situation with Aimee and Kai, it would be helpful if Aimee were able perhaps to voice something of what she has found difficult about Kai being away. This might then give Kai the chance to understand the intensity of the reaction in a more compassionate way, rather than just thinking she's being mean or over-reacting.

This sort of interaction so often happens on the doorstep. It doesn't need to follow a big trip away, it could just be after getting back from work. Sometimes our feelings at this point are raw. The moment of reunion at the end of the day is a reminder of the different worlds we might have been inhabiting (sometimes relating to resentful feelings about different roles, as in the last chapter). It's not just at the reunion that difficult feelings show themselves – it may also be that in the run-up to time apart difficult feelings build. Becoming more aware of these things can enable couples to prepare better for separations, by, for example, talking before a separation about what it's going to mean for them, what it's going to involve, and about how they might keep in touch. It's not realistic to make a big deal of the daily going to and from work, but you can wonder together about how you feel about it and how best to make it work, by saying things like 'it really makes a difference if you can give me ten minutes when I get home to decompress from work', or 'I really like it when you manage to text me from work', or 'if you're going to message me during the day don't expect me to answer until lunchtime'.

Ideas for reflection
- *What do physical separations mean for you both?*
- *What are your experiences of separations in your history?*
- *How do you feel when you're apart from your partner?*
- *How do you feel when your partner gets back?*
- *How do you keep in touch when you're physically apart? Do you have different ideas about this?*
- *Would it help to plan separations in advance (e.g. thinking about how you're going to stay in touch)?*

What on earth could all this have to do with washing-up?
It's hard being in a relationship and having to deal with your partner's views. Sometimes we may just want to do things our way. Sometimes you may just want to be able

to do the washing-up or load the dishwasher without your partner having a view on how to do it. This might be an enjoyable moment of autonomy, even if it is only washing up.

But togetherness is important too. Showing that we are thinking about our partners and our relationship helps the comings and goings in our relationships to go more smoothly (which links with the ideas in chapter 1 about communication). Walking out of the door to go and do your own thing or get some space is probably going to go more smoothly if you show how you are thinking about the relationship. In my mind, washing-up stands for something that the relationship always needs – it is something that always needs doing, on an ongoing basis. Every time someone gets involved with the washing-up they are at some level showing some care for the relationship.

Put another way – you may be asking for trouble if you walk out of the door or sit on your phone with the washing-up not done (or any other job that looks like it might need doing)! If someone is prepared to demonstrate their thinking about what the relationship needs by actually doing the washing-up, this may make comings and goings between togetherness and separateness easier, because there's a reassurance that this person still has the relationship on their mind, even if they are out of the door on their way to go and do something else.

It works in other ways. Washing-up stands for home, for the inside world of the relationship, not the outside world. The rows that take place on doorsteps happen when one person has been out in the world and the other person has been at home, perhaps doing a bit of washing up, and possibly feeling envious of the other's experience. This doesn't mean to say that the person who's been in the 'outside world' hasn't had a difficult day, but the tensions here are about reconciling the different experiences that the two people have had.

Summing up

If there is not enough closeness or togetherness in a relationship, there may be no relationship to speak of. But a relationship where any separateness or distance or independence is felt to be threatening means there cannot be a relationship of two people – you need two individuals to be able to relate to each other. We talk about getting close to someone, about getting together with someone when we are in a relationship with them, but inherent to closeness and intimacy in a relationship is also a capacity to tolerate distance from our partner at times, whether that is physical or emotional. It is a delicate balance of being able to tolerate closeness as well as distance. How as adults we feel about being apart from our partners or about sharing them may feel complicated, particularly if we have previous experiences that make us feel more sensitive about these issues. The more we know about our own and each other's feelings and anxieties about closeness and distance (which may be deeply held and defined by previous experiences in these areas), the more likely it is that we can find ways that work for both people and can feel that the relationship is a resource that gives confidence and reassurance to come and go.

Working out issues of closeness and distance, what we

share with each other and what we don't, where we are autonomous and where we aren't, can feel like one large Venn diagram. If each person in the couple is like a circle, then what's in the bit of the two circles that overlap? What's in the bit of the two circles that don't overlap? How do we both feel about these differences? How do we feel about the things that we don't share? It's in attending to questions like these that couples can become closer, even if that means they're apart more often. Thinking about it in terms of what the relationship needs rather than just what the two individuals do can help give a wider context rather than thinking of it as a constant battle of one person's needs versus the other's.

In a sense, the problem of closeness as opposed to distance goes to the heart of this book. Any of the tensions discussed here might leave someone in a relationship feeling that the only possible answer is 'get out of my (physical) space'. Closeness with someone, 'togetherness', creates the problem of having to incorporate their different ideas and possibly put a distance between yourself and your precise vision of how things should be done, for the sake of the relationship. The comings and goings in a relationship could be seen to operate at a deeper level as couples have to find a way to come and go between their different ideas about things, sometimes making departures from their original vision of things, in order to tend to the relationship.

What seems to work well for couples in this area
- *Treating boundaries around phones and social media as an essential housekeeping issue.*

- *Planning in advance for difficult feelings in relation to their being physically apart, if this is a repeated theme.*
- *Finding ways to show that they are thinking about each other when they are apart.*
- *'Topping up' on time together before or after a separation (if that is felt to be needed).*

5

Sex (aka 'this is so difficult to talk about')

A couple in their early thirties, Graeme and Dee, have arrived for their first consultation. Graeme is telling me, hesitantly, about why he and Dee have come to therapy. 'We have intimacy issues ... as in ... our sex life.' Dee starts to cry. They are sitting rigidly upright in their chairs and I notice that I'm feeling unusually apprehensive. As Dee cries it feels like a long silence before Graeme offers her one of the tissues from the box on the table in between them. At this point there is a lot more to understand about what the issues are that they are bringing to get some help with.

But what I do get immediately is a sense of how uncomfortable it feels for them to be in the room talking about this issue. Understandably so. Opening up the secrets about your sex life to a third person can be deeply uncomfortable. But that isn't the only uncomfortable thing. The tension between two people about their sex lives can feel like the most sensitive and awkward issue between them. Encountering each other's different feelings or ideas about sex can often feel either like a deep rejection or a problem that can't be solved. These aren't just differences of opinion; these are differences felt bodily, that can leave couples feeling that maybe they are incompatible or that there is something wrong with their relationship, particularly when the wider portrayal of sex (whether on the TV or in films or porn) is as something that often happens spontaneously and smoothly between two (probably younger) people in the early throes of passion. In this chapter I want to give a feel of some of the issues that couples have when it comes to their sex lives, and to show some of the ways in which we might try to think about them.

An argument you need to have (but daren't)

There's no right way to have a sex life, no right amount of sex to be having – no sex, lots of sex, sex in a monogamous relationship, sex in an open relationship – as long as it works for both people and is safe for them and consensual.

However, if it isn't working between them, then couples need to find a way to talk about it with each other. It can feel as if it's an area where bringing up difficult feelings is off limits. It's one thing to get cross about your partner never taking out the bins, but it may feel much harder and less appropriate to share angry or distressed feelings about how you feel their body is working or how they don't seem that into you physically or are more into you physically than you are into them. There may be concerns that if you bring it up you are putting pressure on your partner to have sex with you (and it's essential that you consider whether you could be coming across in this way). And there's also the way in which a cooling of affection physically can be an expression of other issues in the relationship which are hard to address: the problem isn't sex, but it's certainly starting to feel as if it is.

When couples don't get to grips with tensions in their sex life then over time it can slip off the radar and become something that doesn't get any attention between them. Again, that's fine if it works for them, but often it doesn't and they are left feeling physically disconnected and with a sense that something is missing from their relationship. Without attention this can lead to problems. This can become an 'argument that their relationship needs them to have'.

This doesn't mean that there shouldn't be tensions in a sex life. Two different bodies are inevitably different when it comes to feelings about a physical relationship. What's important is to find a way to address any tensions that do come up. As is so often the case, it all comes back to communication, and many of the themes raised in chapter 1 are going to be relevant.

The context in which a couple's sex life is set is constantly and inevitably changing – the different phases of a relationship as it goes from something new to something that may become longer term, bodies that change over time, perhaps the idea and/or reality of children coming on to the scene, and the external pressures that life brings. These all have an impact on a couple's sex life and sometimes a couple needs to be able to think dynamically together about how to address that impact, which again is at some level going to come back to communication.

Your body drives me crazy

In order to think about the whole subject of sex I want to start with bodies. Your partner's body may drive you crazy in a good way but it can also drive you crazy in a not so good way. The problems I've talked about in previous chapters (for any of you who have jumped straight to the sex chapter) relate to the inherent problems of sharing space with someone, both emotional and physical. In starting to talk about a couple's sex life I want to flag up the inherent problems of our bodies sharing space with each other. Our bodies may react or get irritated by one another too, each responding to the other at a sensory level. Just as you may really fancy your partner and have a reaction to how they look, you may also wish you weren't bothered by the noise(s) their body makes or the way they smell. Whatever it is, at some level our bodies are always reacting to each other when we share space. Whether it's snoring, throat clearing, chewing, having loud work calls, a favourite hobby involving a loud instrument, or, let's not even go there (okay let's!) bad breath or toilet smells – if our bodies are going to share space then it's potentially challenging and it's going to go better if we can think about the impact our bodies have on each other.

It can feel deeply personal to hear a criticism of something our bodies do, and so we may need to go really gently with each other here (and to work out what we can tolerate – this is something so sensitive that it may feel important to pick your battles). For example, something like one person snoring or having bad breath might cause real problems in the relationship if not tended to, and yet it might feel such a delicate area to talk about. A situation like this might be managed better if conversations can go really gently, along the lines of 'this is really a delicate area, but I'm struggling and I wonder how you are doing too, I think our relationship needs us to think about this'.

Lockdown was really hard for many couples in this respect. There was so much physical sharing of space, and the balance that couples had with one another became disrupted. For some, it was the bodily aspects that were so hard to tolerate in each other.

Idea for reflection
- *Do you know if there are any aspects of your body that impact your partner when it comes to you sharing space with each other?*

Why are you overreacting (again)?

We may need to think about the impact we have on each other's bodies at a more subtle level.

I spoke in Chapter One about how if we are to improve our communication, we have to give up a wish that our partners will read our minds and learn instead to understand their emotional landscape by getting it wrong. When it comes to bodies there is similar work to be done to better understand each other's layers. We may have to give up an idea that our partners can 'body-read' us, and we may come to understand the emotional and sensory landscape of each other's bodies better through the mistakes we each make with the other.

As long as there is a mindset that is curious and open to the idea of there being different and potentially deeply held feelings, the arguments in this area can help us learn about each other's bodies and the sensitivities they may hold.

Hazel has told Sheena that she should think about exercising more. It hasn't gone down well.

SHEENA: How dare you tell me what to do with my body? I don't tell you what to do with yours.

HAZEL: Is it so weird to suggest you take care of yourself?

SHEENA: Are you saying you don't find me attractive when I'm not exercising?

HAZEL: No! That's not what I'm saying! I wish I'd never mentioned it. It's so not a big deal!

But to Sheena this does feel like a big deal. She's livid about being told what to do with her body and this whole conversation touches a very sensitive nerve for her. When she was a teenager her mother had often said she should try to exercise to 'drop a couple of sizes' and now she might feel she is back in a relationship with a version of her mother. Her reflex is to protect herself from that.

If Hazel isn't interested in engaging with that as an idea, then it seems fairly likely that this issue will keep on raising itself as a point of conflict.

SHEENA: I can't believe you said that earlier about me exercising.

HAZEL: Well, I'm not going to lie, that is how I feel.

SHEENA: But don't you see how upsetting that is? It makes me feel like you don't find me attractive.

How dare you tell me how I should look? I think you need to have a look at yourself and question your approach here. I've got enough messages from society about how I ought to look and I don't need you piling in on that.

HAZEL: Well, I don't really know what to say. I am who I am.

SHEENA: And yes I am who I am and you seem unable to accept that!

If, however, they appreciate that each one's feelings about their body are something the other is going to have to get to know about, and that learning is going to be a work in progress, then this may take some of the heat out of the conversation.

HAZEL: Look, I hadn't realised that when I said that it was going to upset you so much.

SHEENA: Yeah, it really did.

HAZEL: I got it wrong. What I was trying to say wasn't about the shape of your body. It came from a good place of knowing that when you exercise it helps your mood; that's something I really notice.

SHEENA: It's just that this is such a sensitive topic for me. You know what my mum was like. She made me feel crap about my body too. She was always on at me. The minute I hear you say that I'm right back feeling that. I can't be in a relationship where someone is always on at me to change my body. You may feel the way you do but I need you to know that it isn't going to work for me.

HAZEL: Okay. So that hit a real nerve. I just want to clarify – this isn't about how I feel about you; it's more – I just feel like it's important to take care of ourselves. I'm feeling it too – I feel really aware of being unfit at the moment and I guess part of me having a go at you is also about me wanting to address something more generally about the way we live as a couple and our lifestyle. I need you to not hear it as your mum.

SHEENA: I hadn't realised you were feeling like that.

This issue probably isn't going away for them after just one conversation and there may still be more to negotiate about how appropriate Sheena feels it is for Hazel to have a view on this. But here they have started to better relate to each other, with a sense of mapping each other's sensitivities and what they might mean for the relationship, so that they can build something up between them rather than saying 'this is who I am, take it or leave it'. Sheena has also learned something about Hazel, which is that she is thinking about her own body and health, and perhaps her commenting on Sheena's body is a reflection of that.

This kind of 'argument' highlights the sensitivities involved when we engage with each other about our bodies. Can it be okay in a relationship to have views on the other person's body, on what our partners do with their bodies or how they look after them? Bodies are so personal, holding people's earliest experiences, both physical and emotional, experiences that can't always be put into words. But as part of a relationship our bodies too become part of the territory that needs negotiating between two people. What one person may see as appropriate interest and care for their partner's body – 'go and get a health check' or ' why are you eating that' – may feel like criticism and intrusion to the other person. On the other hand these may feel like necessary tensions that are shared out between the two of them, where one person waves the flag for care and concern about bodily health and the other takes the lead from that. Understanding the sensitivities that each person has about their body can enable these conversations to be more effectively tailored.

Idea for reflection
- *How do you feel about your body? Are there aspects of your body you enjoy? Aspects that you don't? How connected to your body do you feel? How might feelings or thoughts in this area relate to your history?*

Why do you never want to touch me?
Sheena complains that Hazel doesn't cuddle or touch her as much she wants to touch her. And in fact because Sheena has a sensitivity around the subject and a history of not feeling good about her body, this feeds into a narrative that perhaps Hazel really isn't that into her.

But what we might need to account for here is not only Sheena's experiences with her body but also Hazel's. Hazel comes from a family who weren't particularly tactile with each other. Affection wasn't expressed particularly physically. It isn't her natural default to hug or to touch Sheena. Sheena on the other hand equates approval with bodily approval (something she lacked from her mum).

Sex

When they met, their physical relationship felt amazing. We might wonder about the deep longings they had to be appreciated and valued physically that were expressed and met in the sexual excitement of their early relationship. However, after the cooling of that initial period, they are coming up against their bodies' different histories.

SHEENA: Why do you never want to touch me! Sometimes I feel like you aren't interested in me at all.

HAZEL: Where does that come from?! We've been over this. You know that I find you attractive, I just think we need to take better care of ourselves and pay more attention to our bodies.

SHEENA: Well I am longing for you to pay more attention to me. Can't you see that sometimes I just want to be held?!

Maybe Hazel can't see it, but it isn't her natural response to offer a hug. Part of what she is going to have to see more clearly, and pay more attention to, is that this is what Sheena is looking for. It will help if Sheena can communicate it better too.

HAZEL: I don't do it on purpose – it's just not my style. You know that isn't how it was in my family.

SHEENA: I really need you to know that this is something important for me.

HAZEL: Sometimes you just need to remind me.

SHEENA: I know. I just wish I didn't have to.

HAZEL: I'm sorry about this.

There is sadness here, disappointment that things aren't as smooth as they might have hoped they would be in the interaction of their bodies, that they can't seem to read one another's bodies as well as they had thought. They may need to mourn the fact that the way they relate to each other physically doesn't always hit the spot of the yearnings they have – but at least if these conversations are happening there is a chance that they can become more aware of this landscape and possibly work towards putting it right.

I wrote in chapter 2 about the different unique experiences we have all had in the households and cultures in which we grew up, and the way our bodies have grown up is part of that. Our bodies carry our earliest experiences of relating to the world. We may have been held and cuddled as babies and shown love through physical affection, or we may have been offered less or very little on the physical side. We may have been handled energetically or delicately. We may have come from a background that is very tactile and very physically expressive; one where bodies are on show or where they are covered up; where bodies can be enjoyed in physical activity or perhaps where the focus is less on what bodies do and more on other types of activity. Our bodies may or may not have been respected throughout our lives, and in some cases may have been mistreated, abused or traumatised. The external world may or may not have been a safe place for our bodies. When a couple begin a sexual relationship, and have access to each other's bodies in such a personal and private way, there is at some level access to this history.

We cannot possibly know all this about each other instinctively; we may not even know these aspects about ourselves. Through getting it wrong or feeling differently from one another about some of these issues, we may learn something new, something that will be relevant to the way that we relate to each other physically.

Our attitudes to physical intimacy in a relationship are shaped by the actual attitudes and experiences of sex that we might have from the world around us. Cultural messages about bodies and gender and sex, attitudes to sexuality, religious influences, the freedom with which sex could be discussed at home, the models of sexual relationships between people around us, the sex education we've received, the experiences with previous sexual partners – are all aspects of each other's histories that we may need to become more aware of.

Toby and Monette were in their late fifties and had been together for three years. They had come for help because Toby couldn't ejaculate inside Monette. This was a problem he had struggled with in previous relationships but he had never attended to it – the relationships had usually ended because of this issue and he had lost a lot of confidence as a result. He had been to his GP, who suggested he seek some help. Initially he attended on his own, but after some discussion they decided that as it was an issue affecting both of them, they wanted to work on it together.

As a picture was built up of their different sexual histories and the different ideas they had about sex, it became clear that sex and bodies had been an 'off limits' subject in Toby's family. He described them as uptight. He had no idea whether his parents had a physical relationship as there was no demonstration of physical feeling and he remembered few cuddles or warm gestures. He commented that he had been surprised recently when meeting Monette's toddler grandchild to see how physically affectionate Monette's family all were with each other, and how relaxed it all seemed. It looked like another world. He said it was part of his attraction to Monette – he enjoyed how warm she was, but felt there was no hope for him of reciprocating that.

He said he found it extremely awkward talking about sex and described how he dreaded the therapy sessions. Sex had certainly never been something talked about at home and he had found out about it through conversations at school that had sometimes been frightening or worrying.

Being able to piece together his sexual history and gain some understanding of why he might find it so hard to relax and 'let go' in terms of ejaculation was a relief. He was also surprised to hear it emerge that it wasn't just him who felt anxious. In fact Monette aired her own concerns about sex, saying that she felt less confidence in her body now she was older and that in some ways, if she was honest, it had been a bit of a relief for her to have an excuse to avoid sex.

Putting these ideas together gave them hope that this was a problem that didn't need to be a deal-breaker. They also gained confidence in the idea that a sex life didn't need to only mean penetrative sex where Toby ejaculated. Their physical life could be enjoyable in all sorts of other ways. With this pressure off they felt that they could begin to enjoy each other's bodies and think about how the messages they had grown up with about sex had left them with inhibiting narratives that got in the way of their enjoying each other.

The point is, when things don't feel as if they are working between a couple sexually, however that is expressed, there may be something to understand that relates to their history.

Idea for reflection
- *What messages about bodies and sex have you grown up with?*

I think our sex life could be better

The examples above show how a couple might work at developing a mindset that seeks to understand their own and each other's bodies better, and how they might go on to have a more dynamic conversation about it. This was a mindset that was going to be of help to Graeme and Dee, the couple at the start of the chapter, as they looked at the issues they felt they had in their relationship.

Graeme described how it felt that he was much more into sex than Dee was.

GRAEME: Maybe I just need to learn to live with this, maybe this is how things are, but I feel quite young to be giving up on the idea of the kind of sex we used to have at the beginning of our relationship.

DEE: I won't lie; I feel like he is putting this all on me, like it's my fault. Sometimes I feel like it would be easier if we just split up but is that the only answer?

I'd like to have a sex life, and we had great sex at the start of our relationship. It's not like I don't enjoy sex, it's just that I seem to want it less than him.

GRAEME: I think we need help to try and work out what's normal here and see if there are any strategies for managing this better. Neither of us want this to end the relationship.

Their having come for a consultation, their capacity to even attempt to describe the issue, however uncomfortable or upsetting, suggests that they cared enough about their relationship to want to try to deal with this aspect. This wasn't a situation they were prepared to ignore and live with; they both wanted to address it, and try to figure out something that worked for the relationship even if they were unsure where to start or how things might develop. This seemed like a helpful starting point – it seemed like an argument they were willing to have. They were also clear that what they wanted to work on was improving their sexual relationship; it wasn't that Dee was saying that she didn't want to have a sexual relationship, and it was important to establish this with them before thinking about how they might improve their physical relating to each other.

There were different ways in which we were able to think about the issues between them, and to encourage this mindset of understanding their own and each other's bodies better.

What do they enjoy?

There was a question for Dee and Graeme about how they might define their sex life. If they limited their definition to penetrative orgasmic sex then this might mean that they would miss opportunities to enjoy their bodies more fully. Exploring what they both enjoyed physically could help them relate to each other better and increase opportunities for enjoyment of one another's body.

As one colleague of mine explains to the couples she works with, 'a sex life can be a 24/7 experience'. What she means is that it doesn't only start when you get into the bedroom (even if that's where it often ends). Whether it's enjoying a small brush against each other in the kitchen or sitting next to each other on the sofa or moving the hair out of someone's face, these can all be aspects of a sensual physical relationship. These come naturally to some people but maybe others need to tune in more to what their partner enjoys and focus more on being physical with them. This can be part of the work involved in having a physical relationship. It may also involve becoming more attuned to your own body and what it enjoys.

Dee said that she really loved having her hair stroked when they were sitting on the sofa, or just curling up together. Graeme said 'Well why do you never curl up with me then?'

DEE: I really enjoy sitting on the sofa with you and kissing you but I worry that if I do then sometimes you'll think that I mean something more than that ... I'm not saying that you would act on that, but it feels easier just to not even start that physical conversation, if you see what I mean.

GRAEME: That seems really sad that you miss out on that opportunity. It's funny because I also feel the same sometimes, I feel like sometimes I would just like a kiss or to curl up with you and not go further than that, but I often pick up on vibes that you probably don't want that.

They agreed that rather than trying to guess each other's minds on this sort of thing, perhaps it would be better if they could be clearer with each other. Consensual sex includes being able to have crystal-clear conversations about these aspects. And without any clarifications, often all sorts of unhelpful narratives or assumptions build up and it can be easier just to avoid any kind of physical touch altogether.

I'm more into sex than you

Graeme described how he felt that he was just more into sex than Dee, and didn't see how that was going to change. While at the beginning of their relationship it had seemed that they both wanted to have lots of sex all the time, now she wasn't so into it.

We thought about how they might start feeling desire differently. Graeme found it easier to feel turned on spontaneously, whereas Dee felt that 'the timing needed to be right' otherwise it was difficult for her to feel aroused or into the idea of having sex. She described how if she'd had a busy day at work or if there was loads of stuff that needed doing at home then it didn't feel easy to just transition to feeling sexual in the way that Graeme could do.

Graeme said that he understood that, and was respectful of that, but wasn't sure if that really got them anywhere.

I wondered with them if perhaps there was an idea that it should just happen spontaneously between them, rather than having to try harder to understand what might make the circumstances more favourable for them to feel sexual desire – certainly harder than in the early stages of their relationship. This was a bit of a change of mindset for them, but it opened up a conversation about how they could put a bit more thought and preparation into making this work. Dee spoke about how there was often a clash – she knew that at the end of the day Graeme really wanted to get closer to her physically but that was often the point when she felt worn out and least likely to be receptive. It wasn't just that he needed to attune to her; she needed to attune to him, to reassure him that it wasn't personal to him when she didn't feel like responding to him, it was just sometimes that she wasn't in the right headspace. If, however, when she had had a shower and had switched off from work, and they could sit on the sofa together and see what happened (without feeling any pressure for it to go any further than just sitting and being close), then maybe it would be more conducive to both of them feeling sexual desire.

The question seemed to be – could they be more open to having these kind of discussions with each other? To tune in more to the kind of circumstances and contexts that might suit them both better?

Graeme and Dee had been together for three years,

which was longer than any of their previous relationships. They were therefore into a new phase of a sexual relationship than either of them had been in before. This was new territory for them, to be thinking about how to make this aspect of their sex life work, but it was also, they felt, a different kind of intimacy to be able to talk more about what they both enjoyed and to try to attune themselves better to each other.

Making an effort
Whereas at the beginning of a relationship someone may be trying to be as sexually attractive to their partner as they can, over time it can feel harder to put in the effort – sharing space physically becomes normalised, the other's body becomes more familiar, and other priorities or concerns take over. Part of the discussion between two people might be something about how much value there could be to them in remembering the pleasure they each felt, having made an effort for one another.

All of this business of relating to each other in these ways may seem like such hard work. However, what I am hoping to show is that it really doesn't mean there's something wrong with your sex life if you have to have a more active conversation about how to make it work better between you.

These ideas for reflection cover some of the issues that a more attuned conversation about your sex life might involve.

Ideas for reflection
- *How comfortable do you feel talking about your sex life?*

- *What do you both enjoy physically?*
- *How do you feel about initiating physical intimacy or about your partner initiating intimacy?*
- *How clear are you about boundaries with each other?*
- *What circumstances/timings are helpful (or not) for feeling desire?*
- *How might you creatively manage the differences between you?*
- *What is a turn-on/turn-off?*
- *How possible is it to share in feelings about how your sexual relationship has changed?*

Deeper levels of relating

There may be some areas that are less easy to describe, less known about, that are harder to think about or to be aware of. Just as Sheena's feelings about her body and her history of her body may find their way into her capacity not only to enjoy her body but also her sex life, as Toby's did, so may the histories of Graeme and Dee's bodies find their way into the present. Equally, their personal histories could find their way into the present in a different way, in terms that feel less about sex and bodies and more about their capacity to engage in a dynamic conversation about their different needs and to feel that they can trust each other.

Looking into their family backgrounds, we saw how each of them might have difficulties in describing their needs to the other. Graeme said that the motto in his house was 'never complain'; you just got on with things. Dee was an only child who said that her parents were very attentive to her needs. She thought that she hadn't had to work that hard to describe her needs as her parents had already anticipated them. It seems, thinking about this, that their models may have made it hard to know where to begin to talk about something difficult where they both might have needs. So when they said that they were struggling with 'intimacy' issues, meaning sex, it could be that they were actually struggling with a more general kind of intimacy – one where they would feel safe to be open and honest with each other and have an exchange of ideas. The challenges in their sex life could reflect struggles with intimacy and communication. It was only by being able to talk about it that they could uncross wires and start to develop a better way of thinking together more dynamically.

Unhelpful narratives

When it's hard for a couple to talk about their sex life, there is a risk that in the silence they write their own personal reasons for why things aren't working between them. And because the body is such a sensitive subject, as I've discussed above, the narratives that can get built up may reflect the deep sensitivities that someone might have about themselves. So maybe one person isn't in the mood and the other person thinks it's perhaps because their partner doesn't find them attractive. Or maybe someone loses their erection and their partner feels it might be because their body has changed shape or because their partner actually fancies that person at work instead. Perhaps they've given up initiating sex because they think they will be rejected. Without being able to talk about it, who knows? When sex doesn't go to plan, or when it feels that there may be problems, it is important to have a conversation to dispel unhelpful ideas about why that might be.

Jude and Brett, a couple in their twenties, sought help in a brief lockdown period as they felt that they were 'not getting on' since the lockdown had begun. In the first session Jude said that in fact their sex life had completely ground to a halt. She didn't understand it – they normally wished they had more time to have sex and now they had much more time but it didn't seem to be happening at all; and she was worried that Brett had just gone off her. We wondered about how the current situation in lockdown might have affected their sex life, and perhaps it was more about that than anything else. The combination of the stressful anxious times and their spending all their time together so that they had lost the excitement around either seeing each other in different contexts or being apart and coming back together perhaps seemed like reasons why they may not be feeling as sexual as in 'normal' times. They felt some relief at being able to air this together and being able to think about what it meant for them.

Another couple who were struggling with the ideas their sex life had stirred up were Rob and Connor. They sought help as they were struggling with the feelings around their open relationship and wanted a safe space to discuss them in. They had been together for three years. In the early part of their relationship they had been sexually exclusive. This had felt important to both of them, they said; they had built up a strong relationship and trusted each other. A couple of years into their relationship they had started to talk about opening their relationship. Connor had always said to Rob that he had wanted an open relationship at some point; his experience in a previous monogamous relationship had led him to think that this would work better for him and he felt that the opportunities for sexual variety would enhance their own sex life. Rob had never really felt strongly either way about being monogamous; he felt that the emotional side of things was more important to him than their physical relationship. He was, however, open to trying it out. They had agreed ground rules, including seeking each other's permission before a sexual encounter, being open with each other, not getting emotionally involved with anyone, and always having protective sex.

What had brought them to therapy was that six months into this new chapter of their relationship Rob was really struggling with feeling jealous whenever Connor had sex with someone else. Connor was having more sexual encounters than Rob, and every time Connor had sex with someone else there would be a tense feeling between them in the days that followed, with Rob often sulking and it then culminating in an argument between them. Although their rule had been to be open and honest with each other, the reality of how to do this wasn't clear to them, as sometimes Connor felt that if he was open and honest about what had happened it just made Rob feel worse, but if he wasn't open and honest then Rob felt worried that Connor was keeping information from him. Connor didn't feel jealous if Rob had sex with someone else, and so there was a feeling of an imbalance in this respect; Connor felt frustrated that Rob got so upset, and felt that however much he tried to reassure him he didn't seem able to.

We thought about it in terms of this idea of the

'narrative' that Rob constructed when Connor had sex with someone else. Rob said he always felt that 'every time it happens there's a risk he'll prefer that person, and so I live feeling quite insecure about the whole thing ... I feel like he doesn't tell me anything more than the basic details of what has happened because perhaps there's more going on.' Connor said that Rob really needed to get to a better place about this; 'how many times did he have to tell him that he wasn't going to fall in love with someone else?'

In working with them, what seemed important was to establish a space in which they could think about the different feelings they each had about the situation. Being able to use the therapy as a thinking base felt like something for them to hold on to while they took time to think about what this all meant for their relationship.

We tried to think about it in terms of their backgrounds to see what nerve this might touch on. Rob had grown up in a family where, he said, his mum and dad had been 'fairly wrapped up in their own relationship and their own affairs', and where he and his sister had 'mostly got on with their own thing'. They 'hadn't been there for him that much' and when he had come out they had not been supportive at all. His relationship with them was now 'fairly non-existent'. When Rob said that his parents were wrapped up in their own 'affairs', I had asked him to clarify what he meant – did he mean that they were having affairs with other people? He laughed and said 'no, I mean all their business, their stuff, but I don't think they were having relationships with other people'. However, this confusion brought to my mind the idea that Rob had been kept out of his parents' 'affairs' and I wondered if this was a similar feeling to how he felt after Connor had had sex with someone, that it was replaying an old feeling of being kept out of something, of not being thought about, and a worry about where that would leave him. Rob said that it definitely did touch that nerve, and it was also a feeling that somehow Connor didn't feel he was enough. There seemed to be old feelings about not being valued. While his relationship with his parents was 'non-existent', it seemed that it did exist in a very lively way in his relationship with Connor, bringing to life fears that Connor would reject him.

Connor said that his parents had been different – they had been more attentive to him and his two brothers and he said that he was generally more secure about things than Rob was.

None of this was really news to them – they knew about each other's backgrounds, and knew about the difficulties Rob had with his family. But both said it was helpful to plot these ideas alongside the issue they were struggling with 'not in the heat of the moment'. It seemed important for Connor to be able to tune in to where Rob was coming from and to try to bear that in mind rather than, as he put it 'just thinking he was being over-needy'.

It also seemed important to be able to step back and look at their relationship together. Connor said that part of the reason he felt that they could have an open relationship was because of the security he felt in their bond. Rob said that this was reassuring to hear and also said that Connor shouldn't underestimate the value of just saying that from time to time.

There was work for them to do in relation to their sex life – becoming more aware of each other's feelings, listening in to the impact that they had on each other, and finding ways to affirm their relationship – all of this was perhaps more work than they had thought would be required but was nonetheless important.

Repair

Finding the space to clarify or attend to unhelpful narratives connects to the importance of conversations that repair, as discussed in chapter 1. We find different ways to enjoy each other and to play with each other in our relationships, whether it's humour or shared hobbies (or whatever it is) and a sex life is a very special intimate way to play with each other. But an important aspect of playing is the capacity to make mistakes and learn from them. When it feels as if it has gone wrong between two people sexually, where they feel out of tune with each other's levels of desire, or the bed has squeaked so loudly that it's distracted one of them or the condom has broken or whatever it is that hasn't gone the way they planned, or if, like Connor and Rob, there is a frosty air between them, it may be that what matter is the repair job that's needed to reconnect. Whether that's through having a laugh about it (a sense of humour is essential where bodies are concerned) or through clarifying to each other what has just happened (rather than letting each person write their own internal story) this all helps to keep their physical relationship on track. This again links back to ideas from chapter 1 about communication.

Idea for reflection
- *Does it feel possible to have repairing conversations about sex?*

Our sex life has changed

Having the capacity to have a more dynamic conversation about sex opens up possibilities for dealing more resiliently with the changes that life brings, whether that's unexpected events, the realities of being in a longer-term relationship where the excitement has gone out of sex, or of bodies that are getting older. While there is a lot of information available that might help address some of the issues raised here (though all beyond the scope of this book), the important starting point from my point of view (and that I keep coming back to in this chapter) is 'can we have a creative conversation about it that says – is this still working for us and is there something we can do to address that?' (aka an argument we need to have).

Having babies and going through the menopause, getting older and possibly experiencing a lessening of libido, illness, medication, prostate problems, pelvic floor issues, changes in hormones, changes in body shape – these are all aspects of life that couples have to work at responding to, and which may involve actively learning about new ways of relating to each other physically.

When it comes to the more unexpected and difficult events that life offers up, the losses, the traumas, the disappointments, a physical sexual relationship may feel irrelevant or impossible or inappropriate. The shared acknowledgement of the loss of a sexual relationship may feel like the only connection here that is possible, but that can be important in its own way, affirming that there is sadness that this aspect of life isn't currently possible.

Idea for reflection
- *Can you take a moment to think about aspects of your sex life that have changed over time?*

You're watching too much porn

Porn can be something that a couple find fun and enjoyable and that enhances their sex life – but I tend only to hear about it when it has become problematic. Perhaps one partner isn't happy with the other's use of porn and finds it offensive or a personal rejection, or that it is having a negative impact on their sex life. Arguments between couples in this area give an opportunity to address the concerns within the relationship, but if it feels as if there is something out of control or if concerns about it can't be addressed within the relationship then it may be a sign that professional help is needed.

The problems we are having with sex have nothing to do with sex

While I've been saying (a lot) that communication is at the heart of a dynamic physical relationship, it's also the case that the tensions in a couple's sex life can communicate something about their relationship in general. If it's hard to convey resentment or anger in a relationship (or if it's being conveyed but one person doesn't seem to hear it) then communication may translate to a physical level. A cold shoulder can speak volumes.

For example, if we aren't having some of the arguments

we need to have in the other areas I've talked about in previous chapters, these can translate into physical expression. Unresolved in-law tensions can be a real turn-off, particularly if someone sees their partner unable to stop playing the mode of the 'child of their parents' rather than that of an adult sexual partner. Tensions around roles as discussed in chapter 3 – a resentful feeling of being overloaded with too much work in the relationship (or being too worn out by it) – may, if it's too hard to express in words (or if it isn't being heard), get expressed by being cold or by withholding your body. When it comes to comings and goings our bodies can react positively if all is well, but if there are feelings of not being thought about or of feeling too suffocated by someone then there may be an attempt to manage this, or to communicate feelings about it, within a couple's physical relationship.

In these cases, it will be helpful to attend to those deeper issues rather than to focus on it as a problem that is purely sexual. It's going to depend on the individuals. For some couples, maintaining a good physical relationship will feel possible while there are other issues going on. Just as communication can help support a sex life that feels as if it's in trouble, so a healthy functioning sex life can be something to hold on to while a couple deal with another issue.

Expert help

Our bodies and our physical relationships may need expert help from time to time. When something doesn't seem to be working sexually in the way you think it should or in the way it normally does, it is important to get a medical check-up with a GP to rule out any physical causes. Sometimes there is no physical problem as such but rather physical circumstances that couples need to be aware of. For example, there may be side effects of medication that affect desire, or changes following childbirth. A symptom such as pain during intercourse should be investigated, as should persistent difficulty in sustaining an erection, as this might indicate cardio-vascular issues that need attention.

These conversations about sex are not easy to have and sexual issues may not be easy to resolve. In the case of Graeme and Dee, couple therapy helped them learn to relate to each other better about their sex life, to create a more dynamic conversation between them so that they felt able to improve their situation. However, for some couples, it may be helpful to go through a more in-depth sexual programme. In this case a couple may wish to speak to a specialist sex therapist. Part of their assessment with a couple will be to try to understand if the problem is an expression of other unresolved issues in the relationship or if it is a problem specifically about sex. My colleagues in a specialist psychosexual service work closely with couples to help them understand their sexual selves. This involves working on what they feel about their bodies, what arouses them, what doesn't, what factors act as inhibitors – and then with this increased awareness begin to exchange these ideas with each other through means of a specific behavioural programme. This is the professional body of psychosexual and relationship therapists and can be a good place to start to find someone with specific psychosexual expertise: https://www.cosrt.org.uk/.

What's sex got to do with the washing-up?

Doing the washing-up can be a small way of showing care for your relationship, and showing care for your partner. Sometimes a gesture of care like this may engender positive feelings. Feeling thought about, feeling cared about – for some, this is the ultimate turn-on. On the other hand, resentments about the chores or feeling overburdened with them may become expressed in a lack of interest in sex – why should I be generous with my body when I feel as if I am doing all the work here?

What comes to mind is the clichéd representation, perhaps in films or on TV, where one person comes up behind their partner doing the washing-up and their partner turns round and they start kissing and all is heading in a certain direction. The reality is just as likely to be that the person doing the washing-up may not be at all in the mood precisely because they are in the middle of the washing-up and their partner may have to be flexible; they may not get the immediate spontaneous response that is so often depicted.

Sex is a bit like washing-up in a relationship. Frustrations about sex or washing-up may be just about the sex or washing-up itself, or they may instead be indicative of tensions elsewhere that are getting expressed in this fundamental zone of a relationship.

Summing up

I'm not a specialist sex therapist but a *relationship* therapist, and when a couple feel that their sex life isn't working as it should it is important to think about how to help them relate to each other about it.

Sex

A sex life that is working is a really enhancing part of a relationship; it's also a wonderful metaphor for it. When it's going well it can make the people in it feel good about themselves and each other and make them feel that their relationship is fun and creative. But it can also be messy. Sometimes it works better than at other times, sometimes one person is having a better time than the other, and sometimes one person isn't into it as much as the other. It also needs to be flexible in the face of external events. And it takes work to attend to these different states within the relationship in order to try to figure out what works. And this is likely to involve talking and not just leaving it to our bodies. It's difficult communicating about sex, for some possibly the most difficult topic of all, but it is essential.

What seems to work well for couples in this area

- *Making more effort to tune into their own bodies and their own body experiences, both sexual and non-sexual.*
- *Using more lubrication (or at least educating themselves more about when it might be helpful if it isn't something they already use).*
- *Ensuring essential conversations about contraception and sexual health.*
- *Thinking about when and where they are going to make time for sex if they have children (and whether they need to put a lock on the door).*
- *Keeping it fun and not being afraid to make mistakes or try something new.*
- *Communicating openly and honestly to avoid unhelpful narratives.*

6

Parenting (aka 'this all just got so much harder')

Angie and Jim have decided to go back to a place they went on holiday before they had children, a place where they have good memories. They now have their son Billy, three, and daughter Ruby, who is eight months old.

Jim has been up since 5.30 a.m. when Ruby woke up (also waking Billy) as it was Angie's turn for a lie-in. This morning they've decided to go to the beach, a short walk from the place they are staying. Billy says he doesn't want to. Jim thinks perhaps Angie and Ruby should go on their own, and he should stay with Billy, but Angie thinks Billy will feel better for having some fresh air and anyway will nap better if he has been out. There is some debate about this and in the end what decides it is when Angie says 'It's a shame if we aren't all together for the morning'.

Having made the decision to go, it's then a bit of job to find Billie's wellies, and get them on, and then Ruby needs her nappy changing just as they are about to leave. Billy says he doesn't want to go, so Jim carries him on his shoulders. When they finally get to the beach Angie realises that they've left behind the bucket and spade.

Billy starts to cry. Angie gets cross with Jim and says she had specifically asked him to get the bucket and spade – 'You had one job!' Jim says she was the one who had a lie-in; it's not like he's been sitting around all morning doing nothing.

Meanwhile Billy is getting more and more upset, which then seems to start to upset Ruby. Jim goes to pick her up out of her pram (that they have pulled awkwardly backwards over the sand) but Angie says 'No you look after Billy, I'll pick her up.' Jim tries to distract Billy by showing him a seagull, but Billy is too upset and lies down on the sand. Angie starts telling Jim that 'Of course Billy's not interested in the seagull, he's too upset.' Jim says – 'You deal with Ruby, and leave me to deal with Billy.' But Billy runs to Angie and starts asking to be picked up, even though Angie is already holding Ruby. Angie shoots Jim a death stare. 'Are you just going to stand there and watch?' she says. 'You're impossible sometimes,' says Jim.

A well-meaning passer-by says 'Lovely day isn't it! You've got your hands full haven't you?!' Jim catches Angie's eye and for a second they smile at each other and exchange a look. This brief glimpse of themselves seems to renew their energies and they manage to rally. They spend the rest of the morning having a happy enough time with Billy mucking about in the sand and Jim doing a few laps of the beach to get Ruby to nap and then they make it home for lunch. In the afternoon while the kids have a nap, Angie and Jim crash out on the sofa. Angie says 'Wow, this is quite different from the last time we were here!'

It really is. Everything has become more complex. There are simply more relationships, more people's feelings to reckon with, more decisions to be made, more intense feelings about the decisions, more work to be shared out (and all on less sleep). Angie and Jim may have feelings about the change to their relationship, how they have less time and availability for each other. Now, instead of having their eyes on each other, they spend most of their day working in parallel, parenting ninjas who need to think quickly, on their feet, in order to divide up the tasks and try to manage their own frustrations, only getting a break when the other one is on the job. It really is quite different from the last time they were there.

And this is on *holiday*, which is meant to be the easier bit. The challenge of getting to the beach is one thing, but getting to work when you become parents, or doing any of the things you need to do, is even harder.

If a couple become parents (often a difficult journey of its own), all of the five arguments I've discussed have the capacity to get much harder. There is more communication needed, more complexities relating to each other's families (and some deep feelings about family that get stirred up), more work to be shared out, more implications of comings and goings, and as for sex – well, it may simply feel as if there's no time or if there is, then there's little energy. And there's definitely more washing-up. A baby doesn't arrive with a free software update for its parents to download in order to adjust to the new more complicated world that their relationship now finds itself in, and yet somehow they have to figure it out.

All this is accompanied by the strong feelings that becoming parents can stir up at different levels and, for some, in the context of difficult circumstances.

While (importantly) there are many parenting books that help parents learn about how to care for their children and relate to them in helpful ways, what often gets lost in parenting advice is thinking about what this transition to parenthood means for the parents' couple relationship and the issues it stirs up. This chapter is an attempt to convey some of what might be challenging for a couple when they become parents. This is a vast subject of its own, in terms of the arguments parents do (and don't) need to have with each other, but I'm mostly going to focus on how becoming parents intensifies the arguments I've already talked about.

Communication

When a baby arrives there is so much more to communicate about than there used to be.

- Can you take time off to come to the scan?
- Can you pass me a nappy?
- Do you think she's okay?
- Why is he doing that?
- Look at that! So cute!
- Who's doing this feed?
- I'm really tired
- Is he warm enough?
- Something doesn't feel right

Some of this is practical – 'Can you pass me a nappy?' But some of it is also a way of dealing with the normal anxieties that having a child stirs up. Being able to communicate concerns to each other is an important way of working out what needs doing. Some of these concerns can involve intense feelings. 'I'm scared/is my baby okay/am I going to be a good parent/I really think it's important to do it this way.' It's not just more communication. It's communication about something that they may have stronger feelings about than they have ever felt about anything before. This doesn't end with the baby period. Becoming parents increases the range of things on which we are going to have views. Sometimes passionately.

If we argue with our partners about things we care about, and given that our children are likely to be high on that list, then the way we communicate has to expand to fit. Couples who felt they agreed on most things, or had shared values, may now find themselves having passionate disagreements about how their child should be raised, or about what it means when one of their children is trying to do something for themselves, or about whether everything on the child's plate should be eaten up. And all this may be happening while one of their children is having a tantrum about *their* own passionate feelings about something.

Not only does the communication need to take that into account, it also has to become more efficient. Having a long debate about how best to feed the baby or who is going to do it isn't possible if the baby is screaming and needs feeding right now.

There is more to argue about and less space in which to do it. Oh, and with the added benefit of feeling completely and utterly exhausted, that great enhancer of communication skills. Couples have to find ways to resolve things not just quickly but in ways that protect their children from being exposed to their parents' conflicts – modelling what they want their children to model. The external world of the children, the atmosphere they grow up in, will become the world they have inside them (linking back to chapter 2). If their parents are always tense with each other then this will become the children's norm; it will become the climate in which they grow up.

When Angie and Jim get cross with each other, so Billy seems to get more upset. But Billy's communication is also getting to them and making them feel more upset and cross with each other. There is a bit of a short circuit here, as if everyone is upsetting everyone else. When, just for a moment, Angie and Jim see themselves from the outside, in the eyes of the passer-by, this gives them something to hold on to. What they can hold on to is the relationship between them. The relationship has the potential to act as a cooling chamber for the whole family. The shared birds'-eye-view moment helps them to see what a difficult and mad situation they are in, compared to how life used to be, so difficult that they can only smile. In that split second they can have some sympathy for themselves and get a bit of a grip on the situation. Their relationship is a place to which they can turn for help and support, as can their children.

In this area, one thing that can often happen is that the issues you feel you have with your partner about communication become transferred into the parenting domain. If, for example, you feel that your partner doesn't listen to you, or isn't sympathetic to hearing you out, then you will probably be sensitive to your child experiencing the same. This may play out between you as an argument about 'how to parent' but it could really be tended to at a couple level, as in 'how are we going to communicate with each other'. Of course, how you are going to communicate with your children matters, and so does the climate in which you are going to bring them up, and issues in that area may also reflect issues between you.

This required update to a couple's way of communicating – their fundamental operating system – isn't something that can be downloaded overnight. It can help couples to realise that they are not meant to ace this from day one. Getting used to this new emotional planet you've both just landed on is going to take a while. It's a process – that's likely to be bumpy. Indeed, it's not really a process that ends – there is always stuff to communicate about as the children grow, and there will be new concerns and feelings at each stage.

The ideas in chapter 1 about communication become more important than ever. The timing of conversations, the tone of conversations, and the ways in which we might listen to each other better. Arguments may flag up some issues that need tending to, about which a couple need to find ways to sit down and have repairing conversations.

For example, listening to each other's views on what needs doing in relation to the children can feel really hard if these views clash or touch a nerve in relation to our own upbringing, but hearing each other out is important if parents are going to figure a way through. This creates more of a space for parents to think together to come up with an answer and this process can in turn model something positive for the children.

Leyla and Andy are having differing views on their

daughter Abby's approach to homework – homework being a ripe area for different anxieties to display themselves.

> LEYLA: Abby still hasn't done her homework – I've tried everything – I'm fed up that I'm the only one who cares about this.
> ANDY: You worry far too much. I think she's old enough to take responsibility for it herself. She'll learn quickly enough if she gets in trouble for not doing it. That's obviously what we should let her do.
> LEYLA: How can you not take this seriously?! Why is it always up to me to worry about the homework?
> ANDY: I am taking it seriously! You just get so wound up always.
> ABBY: What are you guys arguing about?
> LEYLA: Your father can explain.

This feels like a bit of a replay of their argument about the housework in chapter 3 but now it concerns Abby (and she's heard it). What seems to have not gone well is the way in which the conversation has polarised their different views and turned personal. Both of them have a strong sense of what is 'right' (which may reflect the different experiences they've had growing up). Is there a way that it can go better next time or a way that they can repair it?

> LEYLA: Look, I'm sorry about earlier, I'm just worried about Abby.
> ANDY: What do you mean?
> LEYLA: I just worry about why she is finding it so hard to motivate herself.

ANDY: Hmmm. I wonder. I wonder what's going on with her.

LEYLA: Do you think she would respond better to you about the whole issue?

ANDY: I don't know. I mean, I'm different from you, I probably have a different solution to the problem. I think she might learn if she gets in trouble for not doing it.

LEYLA: Well, we could try that.

ANDY: Yup, but let's keep an eye on it.

This type of conversation feels a bit more spacious. There's a bit more curiosity about each other's ideas, and more curiosity about Abby too. Rather than them both feeling that there is a 'right' or 'obvious' solution, they are respectful of where the other one is coming from and are trying to find a way through. This repairing conversation helps to get them back on track as a couple and this also has the potential to help Abby.

If conversations get repeatedly heated, and if managing the way you communicate feels hard, particularly in front of the children, then it may be a sign that you need some support in order to think about what's going on and find a way to protect yourselves and the children when emotions run high. Having a plan with each other for how to create a circuit break in a conversation that is escalating can also be important, such as agreeing to separate yourselves physically or to take time out from a conversation or argument that is ramping up.

Ideas for reflection
- *What space do you have to think about the things that have changed since you have become parents?*
- *How do you tend to talk about issues that you disagree on when it comes to parenting?*
- *How do you think your children would describe the way you communicate? (If they are too young to describe it how would you think the way you communicate might feel to them?)*

Family

Our memories of childhood can lie dormant within us like seeds in a desert until the thunderstorm that is parenting arrives and brings them all to life. For example, a new dad who feels displaced by the arrival of his baby realises that it has stirred up old feelings about his childhood, when his mother had his little brother eighteen months after he was born. These old feelings need to be understood in order to be able to get a grip on the current set of feelings.

It's not just newborns. Struggling with your eight-year-old? As Philippa Perry says in her essential book *The Book You Wish Your Parents Had Read* – 'Whatever age your child is, they are liable to remind you ... of the emotions you went through when you were at a similar stage.' In chapter 2 we looked at the idea that being in a couple means understanding each other's family landscape, and the hopes and longings that each person brings to a couple relationship. Now, with a child, this exercise is replayed, as you have to start to understand more about each other's hopes and longings in relation to parenting – and perhaps unresolved issues relating to how you were parented too.

For example, if someone felt really deprived of something in their own childhood, there may be a real anxiety about repeating that deprivation with one's own children and the focus may shift intensely from being a good partner to being a good parent. This can feel disorientating for couples. Without an understanding of where they are coming from, your partner's strong feelings about certain issues can feel inexplicable, whether it's how the baby cries, how to discipline, whether the house should fill with a mess of toys, or how much screen time should be allowed. Both people in the relationship are going to bring their ideas from the climate in which they grew up – the things they appreciated or the things they would like to be improved upon.

With the responsibility of children, parents may feel that they have to take their relationship more seriously than ever. This can bring up old fears about how their parents' relationship affected them. A couple who may have felt easy with conflict may now, with a child, be reminded of the upsetting feelings created by their parents' arguments and they may want to avoid doing the same to the next generation.

Anthony and Michelle had two daughters aged twelve and fifteen. They had become worried about their younger daughter, Kyra. She didn't want to go to school and every morning there were arguments as they struggled to encourage her to get up and out. Even though she did end up going, it was a struggle every day, leaving them exhausted. They tried to understand what was going on, but were at a loss because Kyra refused to talk about it.

Anthony and Michelle argued between themselves

about it. Michelle thought it was just a phase, that Kyra was testing boundaries and being wilful, and that the best thing for her was to just be made to get on with it. Anthony thought that if she didn't want to go to school perhaps there was a good reason and maybe she should stay home so that they could work out what was going on. Michelle thought that would just be 'pandering' to her and that missing school was not an option. They felt that their ideas were completely opposed. They had asked their daughter Iris to walk to school with Kyra but she was adamant that she wanted to walk to school with her own friends, not her sister. They felt that no one could agree on anything and despaired of finding a way forward, hence their seeking help.

It was interesting to me that they had sought help as a couple and hadn't gone straight to finding help for Kyra, although she was due to see the school counsellor. It seemed a constructive sign that they wanted to try to figure this out together.

I asked them about their own backgrounds and whether anything of the current situation resonated with their own school lives. Anthony had grown up in what he said was a very strict family – 'You definitely didn't complain about things and you went to school even if you had a raging fever.' He said there was never any room for him to have an opinion. Michelle said that there wasn't anything specific in her background about going to school but that she wishes now that she had worked harder then, as she feels it would have helped her to get a better job.

Putting this together they each understood more about

where the other was coming from. Anthony realised that he was really worried about Kyra perhaps feeling as he did when younger. He never wanted her to feel that she wouldn't be listened to. Michelle realised that she was so anxious about Kyra skipping school and her academic performance that this dominated all of her feelings.

Anthony said it was as if they were both wearing blinkers and both set on pursuing their own agenda – 'That's probably why neither of us can see what is happening!' When each felt that the other person understood a bit more about their particular concerns, they seemed to be able to talk about it in a more relaxed way, without needing to push their point of view so strongly.

Once they felt more relaxed they were able to chew over the issue together, rather than having to defend their position all the time. They started to think about Iris and wondered why she was so reluctant to help her sister. They thought that perhaps they should sit down as a family to think about it – something they had previously avoided as Anthony and Michelle had felt their ideas were so opposed they had worried it would get too heated. More space for thinking seemed to have opened up.

To their surprise, what emerged was that Iris had some very mixed feelings about her sister having started at her school – she was worried that she was going to have to include her in her friendship groups. Kyra said that she had been really upset about this and was actually feeling quite scared about school and wanted some help from her sister. Although the issue wasn't immediately solved, it felt as if there was more flexibility around it. What had shifted it was Anthony and Michelle's capacity to understand each other in the context of their own family backgrounds. Their having worked something out as a couple took some pressure off the children and enabled the children to be more open and honest.

Idea for reflection
- *What ideas do you bring to parenting from your own experience of growing up, both things you liked and the things you didn't like so much?*

Extended family
At a point where a couple have children, it may be more important than ever to try to work on relationships with extended family, in order to enjoy the support and love they may have to offer. But it can also feel very complicated.

We saw some of this in the Beena and Marco example in chapter 2, where Beena found Marco's mother's involvement too intrusive. Often it's at the point when a couple have children that tensions can emerge around the involvement of one another's family. Relatives, understandably, want to be involved with their new relations and may feel that as family members they have particular access and a particular right to have views on how things are going (or should go). For some couples this won't raise an issue and may feel very normal within the culture of their families; for others it will be harder to manage, as we saw with Beena and Marco.

As with communicating once you become parents, this too takes time to figure out. Trust may need to be built up. There may be five arguments to have with your parents/in-laws about this issue (or more!). How much are we going to see you? How can we call on your support? Is it okay for you to give us advice? Can you respect our boundaries? Can you trust us to find our way? Are there resentments about one family being more helpful than another? Are there tensions or rivalries about which of our families is more involved?

All these questions seem normal within the landscape of becoming parents. It's important for couples to bear in mind that there are no right answers to these questions. Just because one family does things in a particular way doesn't mean that that is how everyone should do it. But becoming parents is also a chance for a couple to devise their own way of doing things (which may feel hard for the families around them to witness).

Inevitably this doesn't always go smoothly. There may be new boundaries to be marked out, new traditions, new ways of doing things, that can feel rather different and new in the context of old family relationships and old ways of doing things.

Even a small thing such as going round to the grandparents to have lunch can bring this up. What time are the children going to eat lunch? Is it going to be at the same time as the adults? All may have strong views.

I've worked with couples on both sides of this – the parents of young children and the grandparents too. Both can feel that the other group is not taking their feelings into account and it can put pressure on their relationship. If within the couple they disagree about how to deal with this, whether they are the older generation or the younger generation, then the feelings can be even more complicated to navigate. As children become parents themselves and make their own new family, the whole wider family may have to adjust. And it's not just parents – sibling relationships can be complicated here and can cause tensions, as different children from the same family have their different ideas about how their own families might do things. What seems to help with these external pressures is to be able to metabolise and process the pressures the couple themselves are experiencing with each other.

Lewis and Bel had a six-month-old baby, Rita. Bel had been on maternity leave but was due to go back to work part-time. Lewis was working full-time and long hours. During Bel's maternity leave she had spent quite a lot of time with Lewis's mum, Julie, who lived nearer than her own mum. She had found this really supportive and they had agreed that Lewis's mum would babysit Rita on one of the days that Bel was at work.

Bel's mum Rachel came to visit and there was tension in the air. Bel had been worrying that her mum might be offended by the situation with Julie. Bel overheard her mum playing with Rita and saying something like 'Granny Rachel loves you just as much as Granny Julie'. Bel had hoped that her mum wouldn't really notice Julie's involvement but hearing this made her realise that her mum was probably quite upset about it.

She and her mum didn't have a relationship where they talked much about how they felt about things. It really preyed on Bel's mind and she spoke to Lewis about it, who said that she had to find a way to speak to her mum and to reassure her that there wasn't a competition between the two grandparents. Initially Bel was defensive and said it was none of his business, but then she thought about it and realised that he might be right. It wasn't easy, but Bel felt emboldened by Lewis's encouragement. They managed to deal with this situation as a couple, supporting and listening to each other.

When a couple have a child, it is a development not only for them but also for the whole family around them. There may be all sorts of responses to that. If a couple can create a state of mind together where they are open to processing what is going on in the wider family, and open to hearing about each other's experiences, this can help them navigate developments and potential flashpoints.

Idea for reflection
- *Do you have any concerns about accessing help from extended family? Are you able to discuss these with each other?*

Roles
The question of who does what blows up when a couple become parents. There are simply (or not so simply) more of the 'who's doing what'-type conversations, as the couple work out how to share looking after a child. Things that seemed easy, like going to the toilet or leaving the house or going off to do a hobby, now become complicated, and you may need to ask each other for help to do things that before you would do independently; even, as I said in the introduction, something like having a shower.

There may be different ideas and a different awareness of what the work that needs doing is. If one person is spending more time doing childcare than the other (as is often the case), it can be that they simply have a better understanding of what is necessary, of what needs to go in the nappy-changing (or school) bag. It can feel frustrating when a partner doesn't seem to know what needs to be done. Arguments around this might flag up the need for work to be done in order to increase awareness of what such work involves. Still, just as there may be different ideas about how tidy a home should be, there may be different ideas about how much work needs to be done in relation to parenting. You may have different ideas about this, and may both feel strongly about it (and you may be aware of this from the arguments you have about it). If the differences between you can be digested through a conversation where both can feel heard, it will be easier to come to a way of doing things that feels more collaborative.

Important conversations about who is going to do the childcare when both parents work can be sensitive and challenging. Someone in the relationship is perhaps going to have to give up more of their identity than the other. There are very concrete aspects to this, for example relating to money, but this doesn't mean that there won't be feelings that need to be taken account of too. A couple needs to find a language together to describe what they feel they are missing out on or what they feel they have lost.

Kiran and Alex were a couple in their early forties. Kiran was a freelance musician and Alex worked in advertising. Alex's hours were long and unpredictable. Their only child, Hollie, had just started school and they felt that it was time that they came for some relationship help as they were arguing, particularly with regard to their different roles.

Alex spoke about how resentful she felt that she was out of the house for long hours while Kiran had been able to be at home with their daughter. She knew they had no choice, as her income was required, but she really felt sad about what she had missed out on in terms of time spent with Hollie.

ALEX: It's not like this is what I would choose to do and I need you to know that.

KIRAN: Yes I know, but it makes sense at this point in our lives, and given your income, for you to be the one out at work.

ALEX: Do you ever think about how much I wish I was in your shoes?

KIRAN: Yes of course, but actually do you ever think how hard it is for me when you come home tired from work in a bad mood and I've had a long day with Hollie and I'm supposed to have dinner on the table for you?

Although it was hard for them, it was extremely important for this couple that Alex's resentment could be heard and named. Normally what happened was that Kiran would feel the full heat of the resentment and defend himself against it, putting his side of things, which just made Alex feel even more resentful. Both roles were clearly important, but the couple were stuck in a conversation that would never feel satisfying, as each of them kept batting back to the other the importance of their role, rather than acknowledging the importance of the other one's role, and then getting into the really painful bit, which is that this role wasn't what Alex would have wanted. What they needed to do was to find a way for Alex to feel that her resentment was taken seriously.

> KIRAN: I do know that this isn't what you would have chosen, and that you are sad about it. And I regret that. I regret that this isn't how you wanted it to be. I do know that there are issues on my side that have got in the way of me getting more secure work. Now that Hollie is at school I feel that I need to look into those issues and address them and I want to do that to be able to help support you.

Something shifted between them when Alex felt that Kiran was really engaging with what she was feeling and when they could start sharing feelings of regret about the situation rather than pushing them on to the other.

Alex also had mixed feelings about being the breadwinner. She had always been determined to be financially independent and to provide for her family, but what also appeared as they began to talk about these issues were her more needy feelings, about longing to be looked after herself, and perhaps needing to work harder to describe that.

As I discussed in chapter 3, the area of the shared workload is ripe with potential for creating resentments, and when a couple become parents and both feel that their hands are full in whatever area they turn to (and that's before they've even got to the washing-up) it's hard to make space to be sympathetic, or acknowledge each other because you're both longing for it yourselves. Or you may feel that you really are doing more than your partner, and that some of it is stuff that they don't even know about and definitely don't think about in the middle of the night like you do – e.g. the jam jar your child was supposed to take to school yesterday.

Sometimes these resentments, if not detoxified between the parents, can find their way to the children – an irritability with them for the role that a parent feels stuck with. It comes back to the need for an internal couple HR function (upgraded to a department now). It helps couples when they are able to map out what they are feeling about the division of labour and to see if there are aspects that can be changed or tweaked. And if things can't be changed, then at least the couple can acknowledge this between them and find ways to show gratitude for each other.

These aren't fixed issues – there will be times where the load needs to be shared differently, if, for example, one person is working to a deadline or is unwell and their partner's childcare responsibilities are increased. Each person needs to describe to the other what that means for both of them – it may not need to be a long involved conversation, but rather an acknowledgement of what extra work has been done.

Other roles
Something I've already covered that comes up a lot in parenting is the different emotional roles we can play, with one person being a worrier and the other being more

relaxed. Let's take that old favourite – how much screen time should our kids be having? There may be one parent who is adamant that it is damaging and worried about the impact, and one who feels more relaxed about it.

Couples get polarised very quickly in this domain. The one who is anxious may feel that they have to up their anxiety in order to get their partner to listen to their point of view. The one who is more relaxed may feel that their partner is being so uptight that they then take up a more polarised position themselves. And so a cycle starts where no one can think about the issue for its own sake.

I'm not saying that there isn't a place for different roles and styles in parenting. My kids always wanted my husband to push them on the swing as it was so much more thrilling and high when he did it than when I did it as I would swing more cautiously! Having parents with different styles can be fun and helpful for children, letting them explore their potential in different ways. But if one person always holds onto the role of being the worrier or the more cautious one, then it may be hard for the other person to think about what might need to be worried about, and so they may then get even further stuck in their roles.

RUBY: Why am I always the one to care about when to get them off their screens? Don't you care about it?
DAVE: Can you just chill out? They're fine!

Dave now feels so irritated by Ruby's comment that he feels like proving a point and not doing what she would like him to do. When Ruby comes back in an hour later they are still on their screens.

Contrast this with the following:

RUBY: When do you think they should come off their
    screens?
DAVE: I don't know – I'll see how they are doing in
    forty-five minutes.

In the second example, Ruby can step back from being responsible for the decision, and Dave can engage with it, rather than leaving it to Ruby to sort out.

Idea for reflection
- *How do you feel about the division of labour now that you are parents?*

Comings and goings

In chapter 4 I gave the example of Matthew and Cassie, a couple who were negotiating how Matthew might fit in his wish to go cycling with Cassie's longing to have some time together. Fast forward to a time where Matthew and Cassie have a baby together and this argument becomes a lot more complicated. Now their needs are going to have to be recalibrated not only in the context of their couple relationship, but also of their responsibilities as a family. The comings and goings have more significance. The balance of autonomy and independence that a couple have established may now be seriously disrupted. In this case, Matthew may still really feel that he wants to go cycling but this is going to have more of an impact on Cassie and tie in with feelings around 'roles': it's not only that they aren't together; it's also going to feel as if she has been left with more work. Aspects of life may have to be given up in order to deal with the responsibilities that parenting brings. What's helpful here is if a couple can mourn that together, rather than dealing with the feelings about it by thinking that their partner is the one responsible for the situation.

This is an area where we often see rows on the doorstep, where a couple clash at the point of one of them coming home. Not only do they have feelings about being apart, but there may also be a mix of envy or anger about the different kind of day they've each had and the different worlds they've both been inhabiting if one of them has spent time looking after the children and one has been out at work (or out having fun). The work required to manage these comings and goings may be harder, with more communicating and more planning needed about their implications. Making plans now involves acknowledging childcare arrangements. Communication is a key part of this. Not just 'I'm sorry I'm going out' but more 'How do you feel about me going out next week, how are we going to make this work, how can we make this fair?' An issue that often causes tension is where one person comes back later than they said they would (or lies in longer than they said they would). These can create flare-ups that never used to arise between them and it can be quite a shock.

The arguments that follow these sorts of situations illustrate the strong feelings that are going on and that need tending to. Repairing conversations become really important as a mechanism to upgrade the way in which the couple approach sorting things out between them and as a way to make space to think about their different feelings.

Beena and Marco had a row about him going out with his friends and coming back later than he said.

BEENA: I'm sorry that we argued but I was so angry about you going out and coming back later.

MARCO: Did it really make such a difference when you were asleep anyway?

BEENA: Yes – dealing with the kids and you hungover the next day is no fun for anyone.

MARCO: Yeah, but sometimes I just need to switch off.

BEENA: Well, when do I get to switch off?

MARCO: Well, clearly we need to make some time for that to happen too.

BEENA: It isn't possible right now is it, now that I have a toddler and a small baby.

MARCO: If we plan it then I'm sure we can find a way for you to go out.

BEENA: But I don't want to go out, I'm so tired.

MARCO: I can't win, can I ? What do you want me to do here?

BEENA: I don't know, just acknowledge that it's hard on me when you go out.

MARCO: Okay.

BEENA: And a bit of thanks always goes down quite well.

MARCO: Of course! It means a lot to me to be able to go out. I feel better for it. This is all so hard, isn't it?

A lot of couples have this kind of argument and it's in

conversations like this, in which their different feelings can get aired, that they can equip themselves better for next time. It will be a work in progress as they find their way through, rather than something that they get 'right' first time round. When Marco says 'This is all so hard' it's a more compassionate way of looking at the situation they are in, and at themselves. It *is* hard. The feelings about the loss of independence can be intense. The sense that life is not as free and easy as it used to be needs to be mourned by the couple. Sometimes the relationship may feel a good place to put the feelings – to blame your partner for the inescapable, perhaps even claustrophobic feelings of being tied down by responsibility. Often the only way for one parent to feel that they have a moment to themselves physically or mentally is by the other parent picking up the slack, sometimes wearing themselves out in the process, particularly if other relatives aren't nearby. These complex feelings can be hard to cope with and give voice to inside the relationship.

Al came for therapy on his own, in some distress. He looked pale and he seemed depressed. He explained that he and his partner Nisha had twin girls aged two. He spoke about how the last two years had been exhausting and had left no space for them as a couple. They were grumpy with each other and he felt that they had no fun. While he had been trying to get them to do something on their own as a couple, Nisha had resisted it. He felt she had become a boring version of herself, preoccupied with the children's routines. He said there was no scope for any flexibility.

When he managed to go and do something by himself, it was always after long negotiation. He didn't mind Nisha going off on her own too, which she did sometimes. But he said it was unsatisfactory that they never had any time on their own together. He felt that he couldn't go on any more but didn't know how to change anything. His GP had suggested that they come for some help but he had come on his own as they weren't able to arrange a babysitter. They had then thought that perhaps Nisha could come on her own the following week.

I commented to him that their situation had been replayed with me and therapy – that it seemed impossible for them to do something for themselves without the other one looking after the children. Getting themselves into a space where they could be a couple rather than two childcarers seemed really hard for them. Al seemed to blame it all on Nisha, saying that she was the one blocking them from having any fun. He portrayed her as a controlling killjoy.

When I met Nisha in person the following week she seemed quite different from the fun-policer Al had portrayed. It seemed to me that she was equally sad and longing for some time together as a couple. She explained that it wasn't so much that she didn't want to get out, she just didn't see how they could make it happen. If she found it overwhelming being with the twins on her own, how could she trust anyone else to? They didn't have family close by who could help out or babysit.

It seemed important to try to meet this couple together. Even though part of the problem was their not being able to find a way to make time for themselves, we needed to try to understand that more, and so we agreed that we would meet online one evening a week once the twins were in bed. (This was pre-pandemic, when meeting couples online was more unusual – it has now become far more common).

There were different strands to the problem. One issue stood out, though, which was the way that Al blamed it all on Nisha – that if only she could change her attitude then all would be fine and their couple life could resume. When we looked into this we could see that it wasn't quite fair.

Both spoke about how overwhelming it had been to have twins. They had found it difficult to convey this, for fear of overwhelming each other. Nisha had dealt with these feelings by wanting to keep everything under control. Al had dealt with them by wanting to get away. When they saw that their reactions were two sides of the same coin, they felt not only relief but also a sense that they were sharing in something. They realised that blaming each other for the situation wasn't going to get them anywhere. This feeling that they had something to share gave them an impetus to work towards finding a babysitter they could trust.

It can seem a trite suggestion to couples who are worn out and just want to go to bed at the end of a long day that they need to focus on their relationship and make time for a 'date night'. They may feel that it is less hassle to share the childcare with one on and one off to give the other some free time. Of course, this arrangement may be the only option, but it can leave couples burned out, drained of their shared identity. It can also stir up feelings of envy as one goes off for some independence and the other is left behind. Both are important – doing something together as a couple and also supporting each other to be able to do something independently. The idea of a date night seems to me more a state of mind than anything, where a couple can, even if only occasionally, feel like a couple rather than two people running parallel childcare facilities. This may mean something as uneventful as the children watching TV for half an hour while the couple make space to have a chat over a coffee (rather than use the time to catch up with chores); or going for a fifteen-minute walk round the block while the doting grandparents get used to being in charge of their grandchildren. It doesn't need to be a grand gesture like a night away or a fancy dinner out; indeed, a night away from a tiny baby may be too much too soon.

Over time, as the children get older, this can develop and grow – but, understandably, sometimes it is hard for parents of young children to imagine a state of affairs where they might have a bit more space for their relationship. What is important is to flag up and remind each other of your relationship, and of the need to care for that as well as to care for your children. Nurturing your relationship by giving it some time is important for your children too.

Idea for reflection
- *How do you feel about the increase in responsibility? How do you feel this is shared between you?*

The importance of support
In Nisha and Al's case, their extended family weren't close by and this didn't help their situation. This often

happens when a couple's extended families are some distance away. It's hard to apply the old saying 'it takes a village to raise a child' when a couple is feeling alone or lacking support. It's not only that it would be helpful to have a granny or sister up the road who could come and babysit, it's also that becoming parents can stir up huge feelings of wanting to be parented yourself. Without the 'village' around, the only person that someone can turn to, to feel that they are cared for, is their partner – who is feeling exactly the same thing themselves! So you have a situation where two people are desperate to be looked after, but are so worn out that they have nothing to offer each other.

It may not be just geographical closeness. When someone doesn't have a trusting or close relationship with a parent or extended family, these feelings of wanting to be supported after becoming a parent can be overwhelming. The old disappointments of what hasn't worked in family relationships get a second airing. For example, someone whose father was absent may feel an acute sadness that their father is now absent as a grandfather so they have to deal with the feelings in themselves and in relation to their child.

This is all relevant to the couple who have become parents because if the extended family isn't around then the couple relationship can often take the hit. The bad feelings get taken out on each other as there is nowhere else to put them.

When I am working with a couple like this, not only is it important to think about these feelings and understand them, but also to think practically about how to make up for the lack of support. If extended family aren't in the picture, there needs to be some planning in order to create a community of support around the couple. Couples have to adjust to finding a community that perhaps they didn't need when jobs and friends felt enough. Meeting other parents with children the same age, working at finding babysitters (which can be hard, too), joining up with local playgroups can all help a couple to weave their own fabric of support, which can then ease the pressure on the relationship. It's also very important to find other parents so that you gain a sense of what everyone is struggling with rather than feeling that it's only you.

Idea for reflection
- *What is your support network like? If it's feeling a bit thin, how might you think together about working on building it up?*

Changes along the way
Becoming a parent is a whole new identity and Al and Nisha had to work out how to maintain a couple identity in the face of what felt like overwhelming childcare responsibilities. This came up in lockdown where home-schooling parents felt they had no identity other than that of parent and domestic servant – in that context the idea that they could be a loving couple felt very low on the list.

For some couples, it can feel easier to sit with their identity as co-parents rather their identity as the couple, as a way of avoiding some of the difficult feelings or intimacy that being in a couple might stir up. Sometimes I meet couples whose children are about to leave secondary school or leave home and they are faced with the unnerving prospect of being only with each other again.

Some parents speak of being well-oiled machines in terms of childcare – focusing so much on how they cope smoothly with everything between them that all other thoughts – including of them as a couple – get lost. Often it is at this point that a couple can feel that there is nothing left of their relationship. Their identity as a couple can feel as if it has been diverted or even eroded by their focus on parenting and for some it can feel like a huge task to rediscover their couple identity. When couples are able to address together what has been lost between them it can lead to development – perhaps galvanising them to work at reconnecting as a couple or perhaps beginning a process of mourning for what is no longer possible between them.

Just as couples needed to upgrade to make space for a new child, so they need to recalibrate as those children develop and change. I think of how the layout and furniture in my home has evolved since my own children were born, to fit each age and stage – the move into their own room, from a cot to a bed, making space on the floor for toys, then moving all the toys back into the bedroom when they wanted to play more independently, and then no toys at all! Likewise, couples need to be dynamic and flexible to recognise and incorporate the transitions and changes that are happening under their own feet. The start of school, whether primary or secondary. The beginning of puberty. The shift from wanting mum or dad to wanting friends. Leaving school. All these changes require a couple as parents to reorient around them. Sometimes it is the changes in the children that cause tensions in the parents. Being able to turn to the relationship to help process those changes can be really helpful: letting off steam to your partner about your sassy tween or shedding a tear with each other about your baby who is now apparently not a baby starting school; having the space to acknowledge the empty nest and think together about the next phase of life. Thinking together about these changes can help them to be metabolised and ease the transition into the next stage. This links to the ideas about communication – the need for a forum where each person's different experiences of being a parent can be heard by the other.

Idea for reflection
- *What does the part of your relationship look like that doesn't relate to being parents?*

Sex
From the minute parenthood is on the table as a possibility it can affect a couple's sex life. Anxiety about conceiving may get into a couple's sexual dynamic, and pressure to conceive can give a different meaning to their physical relationship. During pregnancy, a couple can feel hugely different about sex, which can come as a shock.

Not only is the reality of a sex life generally more complicated if a couple become parents (for example finding time and space to be intimate with each other) but it may be more complicated with their bodies too. If there was a difficult birth and a woman's body hasn't recovered, this is going to have an impact and needs to be thought about. There is the reality for both parents of being physically more tired, and the reality of your days being more physical. A common scenario is of one person coming home from work and longing for a hug or some physical attention and the other person longing for some space on their own, having been hugged all day or having had someone in the toilet with them every time they went. And this can leave both people feeling frustrated and disconnected from the mismatch of their hopes.

While a couple figure out the new realities of their bodies and their lives, sex can be really missed, and can stand for what else is missed now that you are more than just a couple. You may be a bit thrown by feeling that your partner is now full of love and physical care for someone who isn't you.

Inevitably priorities change when a couple become parents but there may be different ideas about what those priorities are. Sex may feel very low on the list to one person now that they have children, and more important to the other. Taking time and care of one's own body may feel less of a priority when there are more urgent concerns, but this may mean more to one person than the other and needs to be discussed.

The 'lock on the bedroom door' is both practical and symbolic. Not only does a couple need to think about keeping their bedroom physically private, but if their sex life is important to them, then they may need to think about how to secure this aspect of their relationship. As discussed in the previous chapter about sex, this is going to take work and a flexible approach: patience and conversations about what does and doesn't work between them; sensitivity towards changed bodies; attunement to what is and isn't going to put someone in the mood for being sexual; and finding ways to maintain a physical relationship even when it feels under pressure from all sides.

Idea for reflection
- *How has your sex life been since you became parents? Have you been able to reflect on this together?*

Challenges to becoming parents

It isn't just being parents that is complicated. The journey in trying to become parents can be hugely difficult for couples and even if they do become parents after a difficult journey, it can affect them in complicated ways. Where a couple have a child who needs particular care due to health needs, this can put huge pressure on them and make it very hard to tend to certain aspects of their relationship. How they communicate about this is important, together with finding ways to mourn what hasn't been possible.

Jenna and Ross had two children aged five and one. They came to therapy, struggling with 'communication', both feeling that the other one didn't listen to them. They felt disconnected and like 'parenting automatons' without any shared emotional life. It wasn't until some way into therapy that Jenna mentioned that she had had a miscarriage about eighteen months after their first child had been born. Both said that they had picked themselves up quickly after the loss and had moved on, especially when they had conceived again. But I wondered with them if they had ever talked about it. They said no, they hadn't. It had felt too raw at the time, and when Jenna became pregnant again they said that they felt there was no need to.

This wasn't the only cause of their feeling that they didn't listen to each other, but it was an important thing to think about, as it was a loss that they had been through together. Jenna said that it had been really awful after the miscarriage and Ross said that he had felt guilty about this but hadn't known how to bring the subject up in a way that was appropriate. He had also felt really sad about it all but hadn't felt he could raise it. Connecting with each other over this pain that they had buried was really important for them if they were to move forward from feeling disconnected from each other. A recent study has shown that the effect on partners is often overlooked after pregnancy loss and that they are more affected than generally understood, with one in twelve partners suffering post-traumatic stress after their partner's miscarriage.

Going through infertility treatment can also leave couples feeling disconnected, where the experience of the one who is going through the process of getting pregnant can feel so different to that of the one who isn't. How can a couple find a way to describe this to each other? Can the partner who isn't going through the physical process feel that there is space for them to describe their own feelings?

I'm acutely aware of those who have become parents during the pandemic who have been isolated and unable to access the usual services, perhaps not being permitted to have their partners in the room with them when they were giving birth or having scans, or possibly even as they received devastating news. These are important experiences to keep processing and thinking about as a couple.

Idea for reflection

- *Have you thought about getting support to process together what has been or may still be difficult aspects of your journey to parenthood?*

Parenting relationships after a separation

I work a lot with parents who are separating, some of whom are separating because of issues they have in the areas discussed elsewhere in the book, some for other reasons. Transitioning to co-parenting takes time and any unresolved conflicts between them are likely to find their way into the co-parenting relationship. If, for example, there have been struggles in a particular area for a couple, then these are likely to show themselves within the co-parenting relationship. There's a different kind of upgrade required to make this shift to being co-parents, an understanding of the need to work together co-operatively for the sake of the children, while not getting caught up in the old dynamics between you.

It's beyond the scope of this book to get deeply into the challenges of being a step-parent (or your partner becoming a step-parent), but it's something that couples often bring as a problem or source of argument between them. Finding a way to make this work can feel challenging for everybody involved. It may not, consciously or unconsciously, be the situation that either partner imagined. Some of the things that need to be acknowledged between the couple may feel hugely painful and stir up very defensive responses – 'I find it difficult when your child does this' – but it is crucial that a couple can hear where each of them is coming from and can plot a way through together, just as it is if the children were their own.

What about the washing-up!

There will certainly be more of it and less time to do it – a symbol of the difficult reality that a couple are going to have to adjust to now that their relationship has been reconfigured by the arrival of a child. Unwashed plates may be interpreted as chaos that needs to be dealt with urgently or could perhaps be interpreted more kindly as a symbol of changed priorities – the plates are going to have to wait, as there are other more pressing things to sort out. Finding a way to live with this new way of life will take time; proceeding gently with each other and with themselves will make it easier.

Summing up

This chapter doesn't even begin to cover the complexities of becoming, or being, a parent, but what I hope it shows is that the transition to becoming parents is understandably difficult and is likely to intensify feelings in the different areas of the five arguments. It involves hard work within a couple's relationship to enable them to step up to the new complexities and a capacity to mourn the changes that have taken place (as well as to enjoy all that is now possible). Working at keeping connected and at being curious about each other's different reactions and feelings may help fortify the relationship as something to hold on to through the different types of weather that parents will experience. There is a huge value to children of having parents who can think co-operatively and bring their different ideas together to try to work out what's best for them. This in itself creates a climate that is helpful for children.

Further ideas for reflection

- *What do you think the atmosphere is like at home for your child/children?*
- *Do you see the children reflecting any of the dynamics between you?*

What seems to work well for couples in this area

- *Focusing on being kind to each other (and themselves).*
- *Making time for themselves as a couple to enjoy a different side of their identity.*
- *Expressing gratitude for the different contributions they make to family life.*
- *Getting to grips with their feelings about their own upbringings.*
- *Where there are differences of opinion about parenting, trying to step back and understand where those opinions may be rooted and what they may be related to in terms of the way each of them was parented.*
- *Working as a team when it comes to managing boundaries around extended family.*
- *Talking with each other about what they see has changed in terms of their physical relationship.*
- *Building up support networks.*

What works well for children

- *Parents who can think together and work at resolving their differences.*
- *Parents who are careful to think about the timing and impact on their children of the way they communicate with each other.*

7

Ending a Relationship

Having worked as a family lawyer for six years, and now as a therapist in a specialist divorce and separation practice (for at least some of time) I have seen and heard many different reasons for ending relationships and have seen these endings managed in different ways. Some endings seem to come out of the blue and cause shock and pain to the person who has been taken unaware. Some are more mutually agreed, decisions that couples have reached together over a long time. Some endings are decided by one person who has grappled with the issue for an extended period, perhaps feeling that they had been trying to get their partner to engage with the problems for years. Some are acrimonious and full of anger, which can be a way of dealing with the anxieties stirred up by the loss of the relationship, some are conducted in a sadder tone, where there is more resignation to the issues and less blame. Sometimes couples transition to being separated co-parents who can work together co-operatively; sometimes this transition is harder and the children suffer as a result of their parents not being able to work or think together in their best interests, or be able to put an end to relating to each other in an unhelpful way.

One of the reasons for choosing the five particular arguments I did was that these were often issues that couples who were ending their relationships had either tried to address, but hadn't found a way through with each other, or had avoided addressing: difficulties communicating; resentments that had built up about roles; sex lives that had not been working where one person had ended up having an affair. (It wasn't uncommon even in the pre no-fault divorce world* to find complaints in divorce petitions about partners not doing chores; these were very concrete documents and so while it may not have actually been the washing-up that had caused the end of the marriage, to some people it felt as if it was.)

I've given up trying

Sometimes, it might be the case that one person has tried to put an 'end' to something in their relationship, or has tried to have the 'argument they need to have', but that their partner hasn't wished to engage with it.

Owen and Corinne consulted me after she had announced she was ending their relationship. Owen was extremely upset and in shock. He was desperate to do whatever it took to persuade her otherwise but she was clear that coming to counselling about this was supporting

---

*The law changed in 2022 from a system where someone would need to find fault with their partner and you might, for example, have had a situation where one person was preparing a petition which listed their partner's unreasonable behaviour. Now no need to show fault is required.

them as they separated and thinking about how best to tell their children, rather than about giving him any idea that she was going to change her mind.

They described their relationship. They had been married for fifteen years. Corinne felt that they had been having problems for the last five years, whereas Owen felt it was only in the last few months that things had been difficult between them. In fact, Corinne reminded Owen felt that she had suggested that they come for counselling about three years ago, but he hadn't been willing. Last year, she had apparently again raised the issue of getting some help, but Owen had felt that she was overreacting to an argument that they had had about one of their children. She said this was part of the problem: that they just couldn't seem to find a way to communicate about things, and even when she had tried he wasn't interested. She said that since then she had cut off from him as she couldn't keep being the one to try to save the relationship. She wasn't prepared to fight for it any more.

Owen said that they had a good marriage, that they had happy times, and that they were the parents of happy successful children. He couldn't see that they had any real substantive problems that warranted such dramatic action on her part. I wondered with him about why he might not have wanted to seek any help and he said that it was hard to think about that; with the benefit of hindsight he realised that he had made the wrong call. He felt that he had probably been worried that talking about it in counselling would create problems rather than solve them. I asked him about the role models of couples he had from his background, and he described his parents as having had a difficult conflictual relationship. This was something he had always wanted to avoid, and indeed when he had met Corinne, one of the things he liked about her was that she wasn't argumentative, that she had seemed unconfrontational. She said that she had liked this about him too, but that in recent years she had felt the need for something more from the relationship and that she was knocking against a door that was always shut when she tried to speak to him. 'Maybe,' she said, 'I didn't say things the right way, but I just didn't know how else to try and let you know how I was feeling.'

We thought about how maybe a few years ago there might have been more possibility for them to tend to the issues in their relationship – if they had found a better way of communicating and been able to think about what was really going on (this being the argument they 'needed' to have). But now Corinne had developed beyond that point. While she felt that she had tried to bring the issues between them on to the agenda, to attempt to resolve them, it hadn't been possible, and she felt that she had gradually withdrawn herself from the relationship. This was extremely painful and shocking for Owen and he needed his own support as he tried to come to terms with the situation.

If there is something that one person wishes to 'end' in the relationship, and both can engage with that idea, then there may be a way for the relationship to develop. However, if the couple cannot engage with an issue, then it may be that the person who originally brought it up loses investment in the relationship and gradually withdraws, as happened here. As the quote at the start of the book implies, the opposite of love isn't hate, it's indifference. While one or both partners in a couple are still trying to raise their ideas about how the relationship should be (which can often end in disagreement), it shows that they still care about it and care about finding a way forward together. When the wish to bring up issues disappears because of indifference, it says something about how much that person is still invested in the relationship and wanting to find a way through. It is quite common that couples come to therapy when their relationship is ending and say something like 'I wish we had come for help about two years ago, but now it feels too late'.

Wake-up calls?

Sometimes when issues have been difficult for a couple to address, it takes a crisis to galvanise them into thinking about how better to address them.

Perhaps one person says they are leaving, but at some level it is a last-ditch attempt to convey how desperate they are to change something. There may be a crisis where something that has been going on secretly is discovered, such as an affair or a debt that one of them has built up. This may be a complete deal-breaker, but sometimes it can prompt a couple to try to think about how things have got to this point between them and to try to address them. Perhaps one of the five arguments already discussed in this book wasn't being dealt with between them and was being expressed elsewhere, more destructively so. This might involve sex issues, for example, or communication issues, or perhaps struggling to cope with the reality of their very different jobs. Starting to think about this can help a couple find a way forward, whether together or through mourning what hasn't been possible. Sometimes the impact of an affair is felt so painfully and feels like such a betrayal that there is no wish to think about these issues; or maybe the one who has been having the affair has already left the relationship and is too withdrawn from it to engage any further.

These crises are painful for a couple and they may need support; particularly if their previous way of relating has meant that they haven't been able to address issues between them.

Getting help

Often a couple will have been trying to attend to something in their relationship for ages and the repeated arguments or stresses between them will be a sign that they aren't managing to do so. I hope that some of the material in the previous chapters may help couples to convert their unhelpful arguments into more helpful ones, but where it seems really difficult to do so then it may be a sign that help is needed to find a way forward, whether to develop the relationship together or to separate. In a sense, all couples who seek help in therapy are trying to 'end' something in their relationship. They are perhaps trying to end a way of relating that feels unhelpful, or end a problem that they see in the other person (a problem that may also be a part of themselves, without their being aware of it), and in doing so to create a new way of being, together or apart.

When a couple can go through this process together, of trying to attend to the issues between them, of having difficult but important conversations, with or without help, if they then do separate it can feel like a more natural outcome, rather than a complete shock to one of them. The ending of a significant relationship is a crisis which can stir up different reactions in the different individuals involved, depending on their personality and their previous experiences. If there can be some processing of the feelings around the ending of the relationship together, then this can help their relationship go forward, which is particularly important when they are co-parents. If, on the other hand, the unresolved conflicts between them are still untended to, these are likely to clog up the way they relate to each other as co-parents.

Ending?

A question I am often asked is 'Is it obvious when a couple should end their relationship?'

There are some extreme occasions when it's clear that staying together as a couple is not appropriate for their safety or health or that of their children. But where safety or health isn't a factor, this isn't a question I can answer. It is going to depend on the couple's particular ideas about what is manageable or desirable (and the ideas of each, of course, may be different from the other's). There is no 'should' here and what may feel 'obviously' wrong about a relationship to one person may not feel so 'obviously' wrong to another. Different people have different thresholds, different priorities, different ideas of what is a deal-breaker, different capacities to want to work at changing something, different experiences of loss in the past which affect their attitudes to the idea of ending their relationship, and different models from their parents of how to deal with issues between them. So no, in a word: it really isn't obvious.

The kind of questions that I might reflect on with a couple or individual trying to think about whether to end their relationship would be:

- What do you feel is not working?
- What is it that you are trying to 'end'? And is separating likely to achieve that?
- What might you be bringing to this problem?
- How have things got to this point?
- Have you tried to bring this up as an issue with your partner? If not, what has prevented you from doing so?
- Why now?
- Are these issues that you've avoided and if so what do you think that might be about?
- How do these issues and this situation relate to your own particular experiences? Do you have models from your family of people ending (or not ending) relationships?
- How might you bring these issues up with your partner in a constructive way?
- Is this something you'd be willing to suggest working together on (and if so how might you do that)?
- What might be difficult about separating?
- What are your cultural attitudes to separation or divorce?
- How are you thinking about your child/children

and how can we think about how best to support them?

My task as a couple therapist isn't to try to help a couple stay together; it's more to help them work out what is going on that feels problematic, what it is that they are trying to 'end' in the relationship, and to help them think about what might be the best way forward. In the next chapter there are some suggestions on how, if you think you need help, you might go about finding it.

Separation and the impact on the five arguments

While some of the issues in the five arguments may be those where a couple feel there are unresolvable problems in their relationship, ending it can itself touch on and highlight issues in these areas.

Communication

Issues a couple have had about communicating are not going to magically resolve themselves when they separate; if they are co-parents there is a strong likelihood that their communication skills will need to be upgraded to cover the new world they and their children inhabit. There may need to be a more active attempt to keep each other informed of what's going on in the children's lives, whether this is what they need in the school bags, what happened at school, why they can't make it to pick them up at the usual time – all sorts of details that previously didn't need to be actively communicated. When there is goodwill in a relationship, getting wires crossed or misunderstanding each other may be easier to recover from, but when a couple aren't together, the inevitable challenges in communication can come as a bit of a shock and perhaps need more work than ever before. There may also be a real need to communicate the feelings about the end of the relationship. One piece of advice from my experience: it's going to be more productive (and cheaper) to communicate these feelings to each other with the help of a therapist than to go through a court process (which is not to say that there aren't situations where a court process may be required).

Family

Relationships with extended family may be affected by a couple's separation. These extended families may have their own feelings about the breakdown of the relationship, which they may express in different ways. They may find ways to deal with their own disappointment about the situation through the support of their own relationships; sometimes feelings can be better expressed through a 'blood is thicker than water' response where two different wider families are pitched against each other. Certainly where there are children involved, it can be helpful for them if their grandparents and wider family can be supportive and provide a more neutral environment in which the difficult feelings between their parents aren't playing out. This can offer children something stable to hold on to as their parents reconfigure themselves.

The reasons for someone ending a relationship may be connected to deeper, unresolved longings relating to family experiences beyond the current relationship. It may turn out that ending the relationship doesn't give the relief that was hoped for; equally, the ending may be a reflection of an internal development in relation to someone's previous family experiences. The loss may touch on previous losses, and how the loss is felt may relate to these previous experiences. These are more subtle and, as in the case of Sean in chapter 2, something that can be thought about in greater depth in individual therapy.

Roles

The way a couple have shared things out between them, whether that's an actual workload or the more subtle roles they play, is going to need recalibrating – often to their surprise. It may be a surprise to someone that on separation it turns out they are more competent in a particular area than they thought, having 'delegated' this role to their partner; or, conversely, it may be a real struggle to take on a role with which they were less comfortable.

Comings and goings

The 'going' involved when a relationship ends can touch on the most sensitive nerves and, as I said above, the feelings about it may relate to previous 'goings', previous losses, that someone has experienced. If there are children, there will be comings and goings to manage and these can touch on these nerves. Often it is the 'handovers' between parents that can stir up feelings about the pain of the situation and the difficult reality of having to face their partner as well as of having to face the feeling about their partner going. So often people say that it would be so much easier if they never had to see their partner again; that what is painful is the ongoing relationship.

Physical relationship

A couple's physical relationship may have already deteriorated by the time they split up, but there may be mourning to be done in this area, given the loss of the physical intimacy and the recalibration of a new relationship between their two bodies and the physical space they share. It can be hard for a couple to shift to sharing physical space with each other differently – for example not going into each other's accommodation, not having the same access to spaces they've shared, standing next to each other as co-parents not lovers, or having to tolerate the idea that their ex has a new person in their physical space. These are factors that need recalibrating but they are also symbolic of the emotional space that the couple no longer share.

Summing up

The ending of a relationship is a process rather than a one-off event that happens when someone leaves or files a divorce petition. Where might an ending start? It may start in the cumulation of untended aspects in the relationship – aspects I have sought to flag up in other chapters. It may start with the development of one of the people in the relationship, a development that has only been possible because of the relationship itself. And where might an ending end? It may be hoped that by physically separating a relationship can end, but it may not be as simple as this and problems may continue – particularly if a couple need to find a new kind of relationship as co-parents. These are complex issues, and when it comes to the question of 'Is it obvious when a couple should split up?' there are rarely straightforward answers. When a couple can take time to explore and try to make sense of their wishes to end their relationship, however painful it is, it can help make the way forward clearer, albeit not simple.

8

Getting help

You may be thinking about whether to seek some help for your relationship. There are lots of reasons why couples might seek help, including:

- You don't feel safe in your relationship.
- Issues feel difficult to address on your own.
- You aren't enjoying each other as much as you feel you used to or would like.
- It gets too heated between you.
- You're concerned that your relationship is affecting your children.
- You can't make the time and space for your relationship that you'd like to – life just seems so busy.
- You have particular worries about an aspect of your relationship.
- There has been a crisis.
- Your GP has suggested that it might be a good idea.
- You are thinking about ending the relationship.

Safety

If you don't feel safe in your relationship, or you don't feel that your children are safe in your relationship, then it is essential that you seek direct help. While I have been talking about some of the arguments couples (need to) have, I must emphasise that some kinds of arguments aren't safe and don't have developmental possibility. Arguments that threaten the personal safety of one or both people in the relationship or their children need urgent attention. If the conflict between you is frequent, intense, and poorly resolved, and you have children, this is likely to be affecting them, and professional help is advised. If you are in an immediately risky situation you must seek emergency help. Appendix 2 lists some resources to which you can turn.

Concerns about therapy

Therapy may feel something that you want to do individually, or with your partner. Sometimes people feel that they want to come on their own to think about what they are struggling with before raising it with their partner. Sometimes the approach is joint. There is no right way but an experienced therapist will be able to help you think about what might be a helpful way forward.

The idea of couple therapy can seem daunting. Talking about these most intimate of issues with a third party may seem very odd or uncomfortable. It may also feel like a frightening admission or sign that there are issues in the relationship that may feel easier to ignore. There may be worries about what it will be like or what will happen. Will the therapist sit in silence and what will I do if they do? Will they ask me if I've had traumas in my childhood? What if I say something explosive? What if I upset my partner? What if the therapist doesn't understand or respect my culture? What if the therapist is different from me? What if my partner takes over like he or she usually does? What if the therapist takes my partner's side? What if the children find out? What if our friends find out? It feels fine having individual therapy but is there something really wrong if I'm having to have couple therapy?

These are all really understandable and natural questions to have and a properly qualified therapist should be able to explore those concerns with you. If it feels that an individual session will enable important questions like these to be raised, then that may be helpful.

What couple therapy seems to me to be all about is providing a couple with a particular kind of space in which to think about their relationship with each other. Sometimes their relationship with the therapist can also be a way into thinking about what goes on between them. It isn't a place (at least in my practice) where the therapist is going to judge which of a couple is 'right', or is going to tell them the precise steps they need to take in order to make things better. Instead it is a space in which, with a third party, a couple can think about their relationship from the outside, and start to think about the dynamics between them. The therapist will be able to see and feel what goes on between the couple in real time, and it may be possible for that experience to be shared with the couple so that they can see things through new eyes. It is a space for being curious, in which the therapist is likely to ask questions to help build up a picture of each person's background and experiences, to try to make links with their current experiences. It can also be a place for letting off steam about what is difficult, and for reminding a couple of their couple identity. Sometimes it is a difficult and painful space to be in, sometimes it can feel playful. (There's more about the way I work in Appendix 1.)

Finding a couple therapist can feel like a daunting Google lottery. Aim for therapists who are registered or accredited with a recognised therapy organisation or seek out a therapy organisation itself. Some therapy organisations are training organisations, so this may mean being seen by someone still in training. However, the student will be supported by the experience of the institution and may also be more affordable. If you are going to see a therapist on your own about your relationship, it will be helpful if the therapist has couple therapy training so that issues can be thought about from the focus of the dynamics between you and your partner.

In a first meeting you can find out how the therapist works and what their approach might be, and ultimately whether you feel that this is a space in which you could feel comfortable working. It is likely that you will be asked what it is that has brought you here, and then you will do some thinking about that together. You will also discuss practical aspects such as frequency of sessions, fee, and what happens when you can't make the session.

Therapy doesn't always make things feel easier in the short term. Sometimes an initial meeting can stir up difficult feelings rather than soothe them or solve them. Part of the work in the therapy will be thinking with the therapist about how to manage difficult feelings that come up.

There are different ways that couples can seek help. Some couples find that an occasional relationship MOT is of help to safely bring some issues to the table. Some couples find it helpful to meet for a brief focused set of sessions, and some couples find it helpful to work at understanding their issues over a longer period of time. This is personal and can be something to discuss in an initial meeting as well as to review over time.

In Appendix 2 there is a list of recommended therapy organisations, which may form a useful starting point.

9

Closing thoughts

In lockdown, a tweet about couples went viral. It said 'My wife and I play this fun game during quarantine, it's called "Why are you doing it that way?" and there are no winners.' It seemed to me to symbolise the essential tension at the heart of all our relationships, the question of 'my way or your way' that couples have to struggle with throughout the lifetime of their relationship.

As I said at the start – this book isn't about offering a perfect-mattress version of a relationship where everyone gets their way all of the time, because that simply isn't possible. Instead I hope I have offered ways of thinking that can at least create a climate in which it is easier to manage the inevitable tensions and inherent problems of being in a relationship. I hope that the five arguments, the five areas of 'my way or your way' can be thought of as points on a compass, points which a couple can use to orient themselves towards understanding what it is they are struggling with, and to help them to see their relationship from the outside.

When we argue with our partners, it is a way of saying

'this is my way'. An argument may seek to justify your way, or persuade your partner of your way, or protect your idea of something from your partner's idea of it. Whenever that happens, it gives a couple a chance to learn something; to learn about what they each care about or what is on their mind. If they can take some time, possibly afterwards, to reflect on these communications, it will give them a chance to digest this information about each other, which may mean that next time there isn't such a need to assert 'this is my way'. (As my wise supervisor said to me when I was training – 'Couples aren't going to stop arguing completely; that isn't realistic. But what might feel like an improvement is being able to recover from an argument more quickly and to learn something from it.')

Of course, it can't be just one person's way; well, not all the time. What the relationship needs may be very different from what one person feels is the 'right' way of doing things. Moving away from 'right' into 'what works for us' (our way?) requires creativity. To make this move, your ideas about how things should work may have to be given up, or at the very least modified. But it is much easier to give up your idea about how something should be if the person you are giving it up for knows how much it means to you, which is why listening to each other and acknowledging what you've heard is so important.

It's so easy to get quick pleasure. I ordered my kids a takeaway pizza recently as a treat and it arrived in eight minutes ... I do not even know how that is possible. But given that that is the world we live in, we need to understand that it isn't so easy to get such speedy gratifications in our relationships. Buying into an idea that relationships aren't going to take work, that we aren't going to get it wrong with each other or frustrate each other, or that life is going to go the way we imagined it would, sets couples up with unrealistic expectations. This may be rather disappointing; you may have hoped for some magic coping strategies. Instead, by thinking about the five different arguments, what I have been more interested in offering (and feel is more useful) is an understanding of the need for couples to be more realistic about their ideas and expectations and to engage with them more fully. Such as ...

Communication
- You probably can't mind-read each other (or finish each other's sentences for that matter).
- If something keeps coming up as an issue between you in an argument, it is probably a sign that it needs to be given more attention (and different attention from the kind of attention it has already had).

Family
- You've had uniquely different experiences from each other growing up, which means that what might feel simple for one of you may be complicated or sensitive for the other, and it's going to take a while, if not a lifetime, to become more understanding of these differences.
- You are probably setting yourself up for disappointment if you have an idea that your relationship is going to put right all the disappointments of previous relationships (which

you yourself may not even be fully aware of)
though it may be able to go some of the way.
- Your partner isn't going to feel the same about your
family as you do, and you may need to help them
with that – which could include redefining your
relationship with your family.

Roles
- You will probably have different ideas about what
work is required in your relationship, and you may
end up doing stuff for the sake of your relationship
that you hadn't envisaged.

Comings and goings
- You may have different capacities for being close or
apart (whether emotionally or physically) and you
may need to work harder at signalling when you are
coming or going than you had originally thought.
- 'Goings' get much harder if you have kids.
- The way you each use your phones is likely to need
engaging with (perhaps more than you think it
does).

Sex
- You may need to talk about your sex life to improve
it.
- If your sex life has changed this doesn't necessarily
mean you are incompatible.

Parenting
- It is going to be a work in progress adjusting to

becoming parents and the way you do things may need to change.
- It may take work to keep your identity as a couple.

If, as I hope to have offered, you can have an idea of the potential challenges involved in a relationship, then you may be in a better place to do the work required to nourish that relationship and to enjoy it rather than feeling that it is a battle of two people's ideas.

This work is not only practical (and still important) such as making time for the relationship by going out on a date night, or working out better boundaries around work or social media. Hopefully, the thinking in this book has also illustrated the more subtle aspects to the work we might need to do, the aspects that are harder to see; work that involves a slow and sometimes frustrating process of coming to understand not only our partners but also ourselves better – so that we can understand the impact we have on each other and make allowances for that as far as possible. This is a kind of emotional mapping, working out which routes get you to places more smoothly and more quickly with each other, working out which are going to be harder going, and how to manage if you are stuck. Undertaking that mapping will probably come from getting it wrong sometimes, from going up some dead ends, and from making some mistakes.

For some, doing this work with each other feels too hard. It might feel safer not to begin the work of mapping each other; curiosity might feel too intimate; talking about things might feel awkward. This strategy can work but risks leaving couples disconnected from each other.

Sometimes there is an attempt to work at the relationship but it feels too uphill. There are some couples who find that they have met their threshold, that they cannot do the work that the relationship requires, and that the relationship has to end (though it can come as a shock to realise the amount of work required to become successful co-parents). When it comes to the impact on children there is a value in their parents being able to do this work and to 'work it out' with each other, even if that is as parents who have separated.

It has been said that a relationship between two people is a 'lifelong conversation'. I also think it is a lifelong repair job – a kind of emotional Forth Bridge (which famously takes so long to paint that it has to be started again as soon as it's finished). It is impossible for two people to feel the same about things all the time and to understand each other perfectly all the time. A relationship requires an ongoing process of repair, of getting it wrong or misunderstanding each other or annoying each other (and these are the things our arguments sometimes draw attention to for us) and then keeping going with the trying-to-get-back-on-track by trying to understand each other a little bit better than you did before.

Is there anything more to say about washing-up at this point?

I took up knitting in lockdown and what amazes me every time is not only how slow I am but also how all those little stitches do eventually add up (even if only into a small square ... I'm getting there). These little stitches made me think of the little things. The washing-up is in theory a little thing, an event that takes place in the background of all the other things going on in life. It's not as if when we meet up with our friends we say 'Oh, how's the washing-up going?' But it always needs doing and it stands for the daily stuff, the interactions between us in our relationship, the little frustrations that may seem petty, but, like my little stitches, do eventually add up. This works both ways. The small acts of love and care add up, as do the small frustrations. When these aren't tended to, they can add up and cause bigger problems.

Washing up also becomes an easy place to which bigger issues and tensions that have nothing to do with it become attached. So to every couple who has sat in my consulting room and apologised for describing a row about their washing-up or the mug of tea one of them left somewhere or the towel on the floor* I beg you, please never apologise. This might just be the important stuff.

---

*In case it feels like you haven't had enough of the stuff you row about at home, there's a post-credits selection of rows that didn't quite make it into the main piece: see Appendix 3.

My work and the case studies

I am a psychodynamic couple therapist. Put as simply as I can, this means that my focus is the couple relationship itself, and the way I work with couples is to think with them about what is going on in the present for them and to enrich their understanding of this by thinking about it in the context of their previous experiences. The idea is to create a space in which they can become more aware of how they behave and respond to each other, and to understand their behaviour and responses, so that things can develop between them from a place that felt stuck (often the reason that they seek therapy). Part of the work is also trying to understand what goes on at more unconscious levels between them, and between me and them, perhaps at a level that it can take time to become aware of. There is less focus given to this aspect within this book but it is an important part of my work.

I work in various different places and have worked in different services over the years of being a couple therapist, both as a senior clinician at Tavistock Relationships, which is a charity for advanced practice, training and research to support couples, individuals and families and which offers therapy in low-fee services to those who couldn't otherwise afford it, and in private practice including my work with divorcing couples at the London law firm Family Law in Partnership. Until the pandemic, all my work was based in London. While my practice has been with couples of different ages, resources, race, ethnicity and sexuality, clearly I have only worked with the particular population of couples who have sought out therapy and who have found it relevant to them, so my case studies are based on that population. There are still problems with how appropriate and accessible therapy is to a diverse population and even for couples who do go to therapy, certain therapists or therapy organisations may feel more appealing or relevant than others.

It may be a big ask to get the reader to reflect on the issues that they see generalised in this book and to link them to their own situations, which may be different in some ways from the examples that I give, whether that's to do with factors relating to their particular experiences or factors such as race, culture, sexuality or gender. However, I hope that there will be aspects that resonate and then can be extrapolated from.

My role is not to give advice – so this book is not a manual. Through my experience I do have a context in which to see the kind of things couples often struggle with, and part of the purpose of this book is to offer some of that context. Through my experience and theoretical training I also offer lenses through which to think about what a couple might be struggling with but this is a delicate balance because what is really important is that

My work and the case studies

I come to meet each couple as unique and with their own particular set of experiences. I hope that what I've conveyed in this book is that curiosity and listening is such an important starting point in our relationships and I try to make this the starting point with the couples I work with.

Some of the uniqueness of each couple may be lost in a book that seeks to group issues into themes or headings, and where the case studies are constructed snapshots that focus on a particular theme. In the real-life sessions and in real experiences with couples there is far more detail than could ever be captured within a book of this length, and, for the purpose of illustrating themes, sometimes things are presented in a more linear or discrete way than they would be over a long course of therapy. Therapy isn't magic; progress can be slow and hard; developments don't always happen in the way you imagine; and a couple can feel as if they are going backward or not going anywhere. I hope that you will see that some of the couples I have presented here are trying to have the arguments they need to have, but are finding it really hard, perhaps too hard, and that they aren't all just finding neat answers to their problems (hence the Forth Bridge analogy at the end of the previous chapter).

Inevitably, just as each couple brings their own experience and their own set of lenses to their relationship with one another, so I bring myself and my own lenses to my work with couples and into my portrayal of them in this book. In both of these relationships there is work to do about understanding what we bring into a relationship and what problems that might cause. My responsibility as a therapist is to keep on working at a process of understanding of what I bring into the relationship with my clients, as a result of who I am and of the relationships and experiences I have had in my life. Understanding the implication of all these and the problems that they may present is ongoing work in my own therapy, within my professional community, and within my personal life. My own personal therapy is a space in which to understand myself better so that I can be as open as possible to the uniqueness of each couple I work with.

A crucial aspect of my work is that I have supervision with an experienced and specially trained supervisor. This gives a space for me to think about the work I do with couples. It is not just quality control; it is a creative and reflective space where unseen aspects of a couple's problems can emerge and be thought about and where issues of risk can be tended to.

Resources

These are reputable therapy organisations that may provide a useful starting point for looking for a therapist.

www.baatn.org.uk The Black, African and Asian Therapy Network

www.bacp.org British Association of Counsellors and Psychotherapists

www.bpc British Psychoanalytic Council

www.cosrt.org.uk The Professional Body for Psychosexual and Relationship Therapists

www.mcapn.co.uk The Muslim Counsellor and Psychotherapist Network

www.nafsiyat.org.uk Nafsiyat Intercultural Therapy Centre

www.pinktherapy.com Pink Therapy – the UK's largest independent therapy organisation working with gender and sexual diversity clients

www.relate.org.uk Relate

www.tavistockrelationships.org Tavistock Relationships (this is where I trained and am now a senior clinician)

Emergency help

If you are in a relationship where you don't feel safe or where you feel you or your partner or your children are at risk it is important that you seek out help (and that you do so safely). If it is not an immediate emergency your GP, health visitor or midwife may be a helpful starting point.

Main government website giving advice about domestic abuse:
https://www.gov.uk/guidance/
    domestic-abuse-how-to-get-help.
The NHS page about getting help for domestic abuse
    lists various forms of support:
www.nhs.uk/live-well/healthy-body/
    getting-help-for-domestic-violence
National Domestic Violence Helpline 0808 200 0247
    www.nationaldomesticviolencehelpline.org.uk. This is
    run by Refuge and is a freephone open all the time.
Men can call Men's Advice Line 0808 801 0327
www.mensadviceline.org.uk or ManKind on
    01823 334244
National LGBT+ Domestic Abuse Helpline
    0800 999 5428
Women's aid – helpline@womensaid.org.uk
Karma Nirvana www.karmanirvana.org.uk on 0800 599
    9247 for forced marriage and honour crimes; you can
    also call 0207 008 0151 to speak to the government
    Forced Marriage Unit
Samaritans www.samaritans.org call 116 123

If you feel that you, or someone you know, needs urgent help and may be at risk of harming themselves or others, it is important that you contact your GP, your local NHS walk-in centre (England only) or closest A&E department straight away, or call 999. If you cannot speak on the phone, and need to make a silent 999 call here is the advice from the Metropolitan Police:

How to make a silent 999 call

If you're in danger, call 999 and try to speak to the operator if you can, even by whispering. You may also be asked to cough or tap the keys on your phone to answer questions.

Call 999 from a mobile.

If you don't speak or answer questions, press 55 when prompted and your call will be transferred to the police.

Pressing 55 only works on mobiles and doesn't allow the police to track your location.

If you don't press 55, your call will be ended.

Call 999 from a landline.

If you don't speak or answer questions and the operator can only hear background noise, they'll transfer your call to the police.

If you replace the handset, the landline may remain connected for forty-five seconds in case you pick it up again.

Calling 999 from a landline automatically gives the police information about your location.

Post credits

These are the rows that didn't quite make it into the book but that feel worthy of a mention given the frequency with which they appear and their relevance to the five arguments. They also show how you can apply the ideas of the five arguments to different everyday situations to help you think about them and take the heat out of potential areas of tension.

You're stopping me sleeping

It's not easy if one of you is a night owl and one of you is an early riser. As far as I understand it from the science (not much) there's little that can be done to change this physiologically. So cries of 'you're so inconsiderate' do not seem to be of much use here. On the other hand, a creative conversation might enable a couple to think actively of ways in which they could be more considerate.

This is also relevant to snoring. This can be a hugely distressing situation for a couple and needs compassionate handling. Words exchanged in the middle of the night may need to be repaired the next day. Where there can be a creative conversation about it that doesn't make the snorer too defensive, it may be possible to think together about ways to get help and to minimise the impact.

In both of these issues we are back to 'thinking about the impact' that we have on each other and trying to listen to one another in order to create a climate in which to have creative conversations.

Tied in with sleep is the issue of lie-ins. In the same way that leaving the house becomes way more complicated once you have children, so does having a lie-in, and there's really nothing on earth more guaranteed to create envy than a partner having a lie-in when you're both sleep-deprived – even if you want your partner to have their turn.

To have a good lie-in (notice that Jim and Angie have a good set-up for this in chapter 6), I suggest:

- Booking it in advance #COMMUNICATION.
- Keeping to the times agreed!
  #COMMUNICATION.
- Acknowledging what it has meant to you #ROLES.
- Offering one in return.

I don't want to watch what you want to watch

Some couples never watch TV together, some only watch it together, some do a bit of both. There is no right way. The argument that comes up more often than 'what shall we watch?' is one that reflects 'I was sad that we weren't watching together'. Sometimes, just for the sake of some time together and a cheap shared experience, TV on the sofa, even if it's your least favourite programme, seems to be a good investment, and may be a good thing for sleep-deprived new parents to do in order to feel as if they have an adult life together. #COMINGSANDGOINGS #PARENTING

Holidays
Holidays can be a wonderful time for a couple and a family but they can also be an intense, pressured and expensive game of 'shall we do it my way or your way', sometimes with more alcohol than usual thrown in. The longing to have time away together and the hopes and dreams of a wonderful holiday can often put so much pressure on a situation that it feels difficult to manage when it doesn't go to plan. Often there are different ideas about what a holiday is for – rest versus activity – and for some there are their own family experiences inside that they are hoping to recreate. And if you aren't in a familiar place, there is the anxiety for some people that goes with being somewhere new and not quite knowing how things work, with its constant potential for debates about 'how shall we do this?' There is the shock to the system of going on holiday for the first time with a baby – a new kind of 'holiday'. The normal division of labour that works well at home may now be up for re-negotiation which can feel stressful.

I am not a deep cynic, I love holidays, but it is realistic to think that there are going to be new kinds of tension that are particular to holidays. If you are going with extended family, that can be great, but, well, it can also be difficult. There may also be issues around different ideas of what the workload should be like, and someone who feels resentful about having too much to do may feel this even more strongly on holiday. And if you think you are going to have more or better sex than normal you have the potential for a full house of the five arguments: bingo. #COMMUNICATION, #FAMILY, #ROLES, #COMINGSANDGOINGS, #SEX (possibly intensified by being parents).

Oh, and the question of holidays brings in travelling, and the question of what time you should leave for the airport, which I have seen couples deal with in many different ways. Usually it is a process of learning by mistake, until one partner resigns themselves to being the person in charge of timing; or they may even decide to travel separately. #ROLES

Timing

Linking into the when-to-leave-for-the-airport debate are general attitudes to timing and punctuality/lateness. Everyone has their own particular relationship with time, and again, this is something that couples are going to have to learn about, in relation to each other then they can figure out how to make good plans in advance and try to be creative about it. This may involve more communicating than they had bargained for. This is also one of those see-saw type conversations about roles, where it may be worth trying to shift the dynamic between you (see chapter 3), although this can feel risky.

#COMMUNICATION #FAMILIES #ROLES

Festivals

I have more than once been asked to speak on the radio

about managing difficult family dynamics at Christmas – it seems to be a theme that is fairly commonplace and whether it's Christmas or another significant cultural festival, it seems to be an area that can stir up feelings in relationships.

I think the main issue that stands out concerns all the big family traditions that people have around significant festivals. Not only a couple's ideas but perhaps those of their wider families' too. It can be hard for the older generation to allow the next generation to create their own way of doing things and it can feel like a pressure cooker having all these different ideas in one place. (I long for a Christmas ad that takes us through all the different negotiations that have to take place in order to get the Christmas meal on the table.) #FAMILY

Let's not forget the 'roles' element here too. Celebrations, whether birthdays or festivals, create extra work, particularly where children are concerned, so resentments can build about who does what, or who is doing more of it, unless there are good channels of communication through which these can be addressed. #COMMUNICATION #ROLES

Driving

I often hear about driving arguments and these seem to be about the different roles we feel comfortable with – can we bear to let our partners take control? Can we trust them to look after us? Is this a role best left to one person in the relationship? A car journey can be a great metaphor for a relationship (two people figuring out the way together, navigating the bumps) but it can literally be a place where two people feel stuck and wound up by each other. Adding children into the car journey/relationship makes the journey/relationship even harder.

We have to let our partners be in the driving seat sometimes, and vice versa – otherwise we would never get to where we need to go. How we share out the anxiety about the journey is important. If one person feels that they have to be the back-seat driver on everything then something needs renegotiating. Can the 'back-seat driver' give up some of their need to control the situation to the other person and can the other person step up to communicate harder to reassure them (and listen to them to understand where their partner's limits might be)? #COMMUNICATION #ROLES

The row on the way home
What is it about being somewhere together and apparently getting on fine with each other but then having a big row on the way home? Whether it's having been at a party or at the in-laws or at a parents' meeting, sometimes it can be a surprise to a couple, or at least to one of them, that things were going so smoothly five minutes ago.

In some ways I like to think of these types of rows as a sign of intimacy, and not something necessarily to worry about, as long as it isn't a nasty or hostile or violent row. When out and about in public we are on our best behaviour; it's only in the company of our partner that we can really let our guard down. Any difficult feelings we might have had while out and about – feeling shy at an event, or like a spare part at an event at which your partner has more of a role, or feeling worried about a child who the teacher says isn't quite on track, or anxieties about a grandparents' comments about the way you've been parenting – have to be held in until the minute we are on the way home, where they are seeking to be metabolised within the processing capacity of the relationship. These uncontained expressions may well be related to issues we need to address with each other, but they may need another airing (or repairing) in a different setting, since doing so on the way home (particularly if there's alcohol or tiredness in the mix) probably isn't the best time. #ALLFIVE

Toilet seats
I can't quite believe that this is where this book is going to end up – on the debate about whether the toilet seat should be up or down, but this is the kind of low-level argument that could really drive a couple crazy with one another, so perhaps it's just as good as any.

All I'm going to say is that if whenever you go to the toilet you get annoyed by the way your partner has left the seat then it's going to need addressing. This is definitely an argument that you need to have, that you need to try to solve so that you don't erode all goodwill. This is all about thinking about the impact that you have on each other, and what the relationship needs, rather than about being right. Underneath your partner's longing for you to put the toilet seat down (or your longing for them to put it down or to stop going on at you about leaving it up) may be feelings about not being respected or cared about, and these are worth tuning in to and getting to know more about. It may be hard if you've always done it that way in your family but this may be one battle not worth picking (unlike the anecdotal couple who apparently ended up in court arguing about just this issue). #COMMUNICATION #FAMILY

Sources and References

My training at Tavistock Relationships is rooted in that organisation's long tradition of psychoanalytic thinking about couple relationships that goes back to its founding in 1948. However, it's rare that in the consulting room with clients I refer to theory or to an academic paper, even though the theory that I have learned in my training and working underpins what I do. The atmosphere of my work isn't really like that, being more informal and practical. Similarly, this book isn't full of theoretical information or references to academic papers as I've wanted to create an informal and accessible atmosphere for thinking about our intimate personal lives. For the purposes of this section I'm going to list here the texts and resources that have particularly inspired me or helped me with writing this book.

Alison Andrew, Sarah Cattan, Monica Costa Dias, Christine Farquharson, Lucy Kraftman, Sonya Krutikova, Angus Phimister and Almudena Sevilla: briefing note from the Institute for Fiscal Studies on 27 May 2020 (referenced in chapter 3), p. 27.

Andrew Balfour, Mary Morgan and Christopher Vincent, *How Couple Relationships Shape Our World* (Karnac, 2021).

Andrew Balfour, 'Between partnering and parenting: psychoanalytic approaches to working with parental couples', *Psychoanalytic Psychotherapy*, 35:4 (2021), pp. 396–411.

Sources and References

Ronald Britton, 'Narcissistic problems in sharing space', in *Sex, Death, and the Superego* (Karnac, 2003).

Warren Colman, in Stanley Ruszczynski, *Psychotherapy with Couples – Theory and Practice at the Tavistock Institute of Marital Studies* (Karnac, 1993), chapter 5. The quote in the closing thoughts about marriage as a 'lifelong conversation' comes from this chapter, which was helpful to me in writing Chapter 2.

Christopher Clulow and Janet Mattinson, *Marriage Inside Out – Understanding Problems of Intimacy* (Penguin, 1989).

Christopher Clulow, *Adult Attachment and Couple Psychotherapy* (Routledge, 2001).

Christopher Clulow and Christopher Vincent, *In the Child's Best Interests? Divorce Court Welfare and the Search for a Settlement* (Tavistock/Sweet and Maxwell, 1987).

Henry V. Dicks, *Marital tensions – clinical studies towards a psychological theory of interactions* (Routledge & Kegan Paul, 1967).

Duncan, C., Ryan, G., Moller, N. P., & Davies, R. (2020). 'Who attends couples counselling in the UK and why?' *Journal of Sex & Marital Therapy*, 46(2), 177–186.

Gordon Harold, et al., *What works to enhance interparental relationships and improve outcomes for children* (EIF, 2016).

Gordon T. Harold and Ruth Sellers, 'Annual Research Review: interparental conflict and youth psychopathology: an evidence review and practice focused update', *Journal of Child Psychology and Psychiatry*, 59:4 (2018), pp. 374–402.

Damian McCann, *Same-Sex Couples and Other Identities: Psychoanalytic Perspectives* (Routledge, 2022).

Mary Morgan, *A Couple State of Mind – Psychoanalysis of Couples and the Tavistock Relationships Model* (Routledge, 2019).

Aleksandra Novakovic, *Couple Dynamics – Psychoanalytic Perspectives in Work with the Individual, the Couple and the Group* (Karnac, 2016).

Carolyn Pape Cowan and Philip A. Cowan, *When Partners Become Parents – The Big Life Change for Couples* (Routledge, 1999).

Five Arguments All Couples (Need To) Have

Philippa Perry, *The Book You Wish Your Parents Had Read (and Your Children Will be Glad That You Did)* (Penguin, 2019).

Sasha Roseneil, Isabel Crowhurst, Tone Hellesund, Ana Cristina Santos and Mariya Stoilova, *The Tenacity of the Couple-Norm* (UCL Press, 2020).

Stanley Ruszczynski, *Psychotherapy with Couples – Theory and Practice at the Tavistock Institute of Marital Studies* (Karnac, 1993).

Avi Shmueli, 'Working therapeutically with high conflict divorce', in Balfour, et al., *How Couple Relationships Shape Our World* (2012), chapter 5. He describes a couple who always argue over when to wash a teaspoon. This idea clearly influenced me greatly! He uses this example to illustrate how 'certain arguments between couples become repetitive because they represent important underlying themes for one or both of them'. His thinking about divorce in this chapter is also relevant to the chapter about ending relationships.

Blake Spears and Lanz Lowen, *Choices – Perspectives of Gay Men on Monogamy, Non-monogamy, and Marriage* (Create Space, 2016).

Margot Waddell, *Inside Lives – Psychoanalysis and the Growth of the Personality* (Routledge, 2002).

Understanding Your Child Series (Jessica Kingsley Publishers with The Tavistock Clinic)

D. W. Winnicott, *The Child, the Family and the Outside World* (1964; reprinted Penguin Books, 1991).

https://www.imperial.ac.uk/news/206373/post-traumatic-stress-experienced-partners-following-miscarriage/

The tweet that went viral referred to in the closing thoughts is from the account of Eric Spiegelman @ericspiegelman: 'My wife and I play this fun game during quarantine, it's called "Why Are You Doing It That Way?" and there are no winners': 6.24 p.m., 4 April 2020.

Further reading/helpful links to look at specifically in the area of couple relationships or therapy:

www.seeitdifferently.org. This is an amazing website with videos that highlight how children can get lost when their parents are stuck in poorly resolved conflict and it gives ideas on how to do things differently when arguments escalate.

The Shackleton Relationships Project: In this project couples who had been interviewed periodically since marriage were interviewed in their tenth year of marriage as were married or unmarried and heterosexual or same-sex couples of fifteen to thirty years' duration. By doing so, the research team gained valuable insights into what drives thriving, enduring relationships across the course of a life and proposed ten 'critical' questions that couples should ask before embarking on a serious relationship in order to help them thrive.

http://socialsciences.exeter.ac.uk/media/universityofexeter/ collegeofsocialsciencesandinternationalstudies/lawimages/ familyregulationandsociety/shackletonproject/Shackleton_ ReportFinal.pdf

If you have enjoyed reading about therapy in what I hope has been an accessible way, then I recommend anything by Susie Orbach, Philippa Perry or Julia Samuel – these are all essential reads. Alain de Botton, *The Course of Love* (Penguin, 2016), is also a wonderful and informative read about couple relationships and Susannah Abse's book *Tell Me the Truth About Love* (Ebury, 2022) paints a vivid and rich picture of the process of couple therapy.

In all of the above I apologise for any omissions or errors of acknowledgement.

Acknowledgements

You may have gathered that I am big on acknowledgement ... so this is an important section to me. Needless to say, I am sorry if I forget someone and I suspect in most cases my words won't convey the depth of gratitude or the depth of help that has been offered. In fact, it's hard to know where to start or to stop. So many conversations and experiences with friends, acquaintances and people around me have rubbed off in their own way and shaped my thinking, and so many people have supported me. I will never look at a book the same way now I know how much help and reliance on people is involved in making it (or maybe it's just me).

The idea for the book came up over lunch with friends – all of us frazzled and worn out with toddlers and talking about how we were all arguing about the same things. It was my husband Rupert who suggested that I turned the conversation into a book. He is the one who kept on at me to do it, who helped me to believe that I could, and he and our relationship is the reason this book has been possible in so many ways.

Turning an idea into a reality was made possible by my fabulous, calm and highly skilled agent, Charlotte Merritt. She is just so cool and committed, adeptly negotiating my publishing deal while I lay in bed with an early bout of Covid, and always being there for me. Thank you too to all the team at Andrew Nurnberg – your selling the book in different countries is mindblowing and exciting.

Acknowledgements

I had no idea how to write a book. Thank you to Helen Conford who initially took the book on at Profile for her wise words about how to start. Thank you to James Rebanks and and Kathyrn Aalto whose online writing course gave me confidence and inspiration. Thank you more than anyone in this regard to Rebecca Gray, my publisher at Profile, who has been such a skilful, warm, fun and funny editor. I have felt always in such good company and in such good hands with your thoughts and comments and confidence.

On that note thank you so much to all the team at Profile. You have all been so friendly and expert. Anna-Marie Fitzgerald, thank you for all your hard work and brilliance on the publicity side. Penny Daniel, thank you for taking care of everything and being patient with me, and Penny Gardiner, thank you for your adept copy editing. Thank you for your hard work on my behalf Calah Singleton and Zara Sehr Ashraf. Thank you Anna Morrison and Steve Panton for the cover. And thank you Nathaniel McKenzie for your work on the audiobook.

I am so grateful to Tavistock Relationships and to all my colleagues there so there's lots of thanks here. The years of client work and supervision and training and meetings and conversations in kitchens and corridors and now on Zoom are really the foundation stones of this book. Thank you to everyone in the Clinical teams, in the Appointments and Allocations and Reception teams, I really appreciate all that you do and have done to make the work with clients possible and to create the setting. Thank you Heather Williamson for professionalism, support and laughs over many years, and thank you to Sam Ahmad, Vanessa Kearns, Mandip Matharu and Andrea Schuller, for all that you have handled in relation to my work over the years. Thank you too to Clare Chisholm and all the Admin and Finance team – there is so much you do behind the scenes that makes the work with clients possible. Thank you John Fenna for giving me opportunities to write about couples and to start to develop that side of my work. To my chief exec Andrew Balfour, thank you for leading the TR ship and creating an environment in which it is possible to write a book like this and feel good about it. Thank you for taking the time to read it and comment and help me with it and for being so encouraging about my writing. Damian McCann and David Hewison, thank you for helping me think about some of the complex issues that I needed to address when writing. Thank you Honor Rhodes and Kate Thompson for your generous encouragement in relation to the book. And thank you Limor Abramov and Judith Jamieson for all your support over the years.

Thank you to Janet Newman, Sarah Vicary and Preethika Chandra – you were my supervision colleagues in the 'formative years' of this book and your warmth, humour and commitment to your work has been an inspiration to me. Thank you all of you for your comments and time spent reading and for your friendship and kindness. Indeed, thank you to all my supervision colleagues and supervisors over the years – I have learned and keep learning so much from you all. Thank you to John Goodchild who is my training supervisor referred to in the closing thoughts.

Thank you to my TR supervisor Jean Pennant – this book really couldn't have happened without you. The ideas in it have all been developed in the years spent in your supervision group and a lot of them are yours. I hope that my writing this book can go some way to conveying the deep gratitude that I feel to you for the working life you have made possible for me. I am so grateful for the style and way of working that you have modelled and that I try to aspire to and have tried to convey in my writing. You manage to combine warmth, wisdom, humour and kindness with rigorous theoretical underpinning. You are never judgemental nor do you let us take ourselves too seriously. I hope this book does some justice to your ideas. Thank you also for your specific comments on chapter 5.

Thank you to Avi Shmueli, you have helped me and this book grow in many ways, not just with the teaspoon couple! And thanks for your help with chapter 7. Thank you to Liz Hamlin, my private supervisor for helping me develop my practice and myself. Together you two have really brought me up in how to think about divorce and separation, and you've helped me grow up a bit and believe in myself.

To everyone at FLIP (Family Law in Partnership) – thank you for all your support, your wise and innovative approach to divorce and separation, and your good sense of fun. Becoming part of your team and having the chance to think with you and work on

Acknowledgements

communicating important issues together has been a place I have felt able to develop and grow in confidence and that has helped this book come to life. Thanks too for bearing with me while I worked on it, I really appreciate it. In particular, a big thanks must go to Wendy Hoare, who keeps the show on the road for me and works so hard in so many ways.

Thank you to Laura Gibbons – you were there for me as a friend and as a colleague, taking on the supervision of my fictional case studies, an experiment which felt like an important and creative process as part of the development of the book. Thank you for reading the manuscript and for keeping me going with your kindness, patience and clarity of insight. I value our friendship so much, there is always something to say, and never enough time. Thank you Krisztina Glausius for reading the manuscript and offering your kindness and wisdom and sense of humour. Thank you Rachel Kelly for so much wisdom, good advice and generosity. It is special to share this with you. Thank you Susie Orbach – you are a role model and you have been so inspiring and kind to me over the years and your books have had a huge impact on me.

The aforementioned bout of Covid turned into something longer than hoped and combined with the pressures of homeschooling wasn't exactly the calm or energised setting I had imagined in which to sit down and write. I have a number of people to thank for making it vaguely possible to get to my desk. First, my family – thank you for bearing with me, homeschooling and lockdown was so hard, and made harder by having a mum/wife with a heavy head full of ideas that needed to be written down but weren't and the pressure of a deadline to meet. Thank you to the wonderful teachers who helped my kids through homeschooling – this helped me too. The role you do as teachers is everything in terms of our own adult mental health and creativity. Thank you Freddie Booth for helping too at this point.

I hadn't realised how hard it would be to find and create the physical and mental space I needed to write by extricating myself from responsibilities. It involved relying on so many people for their help and goodwill. Thank you Rohan Silva for the offer of a desk at Second Home in the early days pre-lockdown when I realised that writing at the kitchen table was a disastrous plan. Fay, Rosana, Natasha, Michelle, Becky, Lisa – all the things (including pets!) that you took care of at different times on my behalf made valuable space for me. The support in the school communities around my children was huge, and I'm grateful for you bearing with me (and looking after my children at times!) while I kept on at this work.

Thank you to my psychoanalyst Dr Bernard Roberts for your care and insight. You've helped me clarify and understand what this book is all about. It turns out I really quite enjoy writing, and I'm very grateful to you for helping me resolve the 'arguments I needed to have with myself' to be able to do it.

To all my wonderful friends – you've all carried me through this process with your patience and support, both moral and practical. The many conversations with you over the years and the rich experiences with you and your families have taught me so much and been so supportive and some of you have given me really helpful angles on particular subjects or gone out of your way to help me. Talking with you is the ultimate luxury and I've missed you while I've had my head down.

Thank you to my extended family in which I include my in-laws for all the support and love and experiences and all the different models of relationships you've shown me which have helped shape my thinking and helped me develop. In particular, thank you to my mum – I couldn't do it without you. Thank you for the love you give us now and for all the love you have given over so many years.

Thank you to my children and to my husband Rupert. This book has been a labour of love and you are the people who have made that possible – I love you all so much and while it was excruciating at times taking myself away from you to actually do this, the hard work was possible because of wanting to do it for you. Thank you Rupert for teaching me more about relationships than anyone, and for doing the bins, and all the other stuff too. There's no one I'd rather argue with.

Thank you finally to the clients I have worked with over the years. Thank you for showing up, taking the plunge into therapy, and for being up for thinking and working together. I have really deeply enjoyed working with you and I consider it a privilege.